Hope for Ever

The Christian View
of Life and Death

Didsbury Lectures, 2004

Hope for Ever

The Christian View of Life and Death

Stephen S. Smalley

PATERNOSTER

Copyright © 2005 Stephen S. Smalley
First published in 2005 by Paternoster Press

11 10 09 08 07 06 05   7 6 5 4 3 2 1

Paternoster Press is an imprint of Authentic Media,
9 Holdom Avenue, Bletchley, Milton Keynes MK1 1QR, UK
and
P.O. Box 1047, Waynesboro, GA 30830-2047, USA

www.authenticmedia.co.uk/paternoster

British Library Cataloguing in Publication Data
A catalogue record for this book is available from the British Library

ISBN 1-84227-358-2

Cover Design by FourNineZero
Typeset by WestKey Ltd, Falmouth, Cornwall
Print Management by Adare Carwin
Printed by J. H. Haynes & Co. Ltd, Sparkford

This book is for all my theological students,
past and present.

In hope.

Contents

Preface

The four chapters in this book originally formed the 2004 Didsbury Lectures, which were delivered in the Nazarene Theological College, Manchester. I am very glad to have been associated with that distinguished institution, in varying capacities, during my time in Chester; and I should like to thank the Principal and Faculty of the College for so kindly inviting me to undertake this project, and for their generous hospitality on that occasion.

'Hope', in relation to life and death, is on any showing a topic of great importance. Its wide relevance and pastoral implications are obvious, although I do not claim, by any means, to have answered all the questions that are raised by the issue. I have simply tried, as a biblical theologian and in a quest for truth, to set out with honesty what I take to be the Christian content of the subject.

I am grateful to those who were present at each of the Lectures for the warmth with which they received the presentations, and in particular for the open response they gave to the more debatable aspects of my conclusions about the nature of eternal hope.

Stephen Smalley
The Feast of the Transfiguration 2004

Abbreviations

AB	Anchor Bible Series
Adam and Eve (Apoc)	*Life of Adam and Eve (Apocalypse)*
Adam and Eve (Vita)	*(Life)*
Asc. Isa.	*Martyrdom and Ascension of Isaiah the Prophet*
BDAG	F.W. Danker (ed.), *A Greek-English Lexicon of the New Testament and other Early Christian Literature* (3rd edn.; Chicago/London: University of Chicago Press, 2000)
BNTC	Black's New Testament Commentaries Series
BTDNT	G. Kittel and G. Friedrich (ed.), *Theological Dictionary of the New Testament* (abbr. G.W. Bromiley; Grand Rapids/Exeter: Eerdmans/Paternoster Press, 1985)
EvQ	*Evangelical Quarterly*
IBD	N. Hillyer (ed.), *The Illustrated Bible Dictionary* (3 vols.; Leicester: Inter-Varsity Press, 1980)
Ignatius, *Rom.*	Ignatius, *Letter to the Romans*
Jos. Asen.	*Joseph and Aseneth*
Josephus, *Ant.*	Josephus, *Antiquities*
LXX	Septuagint
MNTC	Moffatt New Testament Commentary Series
NCB	New Century Bible Series

NIDNTT	C. Brown (ed.), *The New International Dictionary of New Testament Theology* (3 vols. Grand Rapids/Exeter: Zondervan/ Paternoster Press, 1975–78)
NIGTC	New International Greek Testament Commentary Series
NJB	The New Jerusalem Bible
OBC	J. Barton and J. Muddiman (eds.), *The Oxford Bible Commentary* (Oxford/New York: Oxford University Press, 2001)
Origen, *Con. Cels.*	Origen, *Contra Celsum (Against Celsus)*
PBTM	Paternoster Biblical and Theological Monographs Series
SBT	Studies in Biblical Theology Series
SNTSMS	Society for New Testament Studies Monograph Series
TNTC	Tyndale New Testament Commentaries Series
WBC	Word Biblical Commentary Series

1

The God of Hope

God's Future

The theological virtue of hope 'is a matter of central concern for a credible articulation of Christian belief, which must seek a total understanding of God and God's purposes, capable of embracing not only the possibilities of the present but also the sufferings of the past and the expectations of the future'.[1] John Polkinghorne's passionate conviction provides us with a valuable introduction to the many-sided subject of hope, our main theme in these reflections on the Christian view of life and death. For hope forms part of every dimension of human existence, sacred and secular, here and (in the religious scheme) hereafter.

Hope seeks to make sense of history, with its evil and suffering as well as its good. Moreover, the topic forces any believer to give a full account of God, the Father of our Lord Jesus Christ. God is perceived accordingly not simply as Mind behind a cosmic order, but as the Lord who is sovereign and active in his creation; and his Christ must be regarded in this context not merely as an inspired teacher, but also as the Saviour of the world.[2] The doctrine of hope

---

[1] J. Polkinghorne, *The God of Hope and the End of the World* (London: SPCK, 2002), 93.
[2] John 4:42; 1 John 4:14. Cf. Polkinghorne, *God of Hope*, 94–95.

pushes enquirers to the intellectual and spiritual limits of theological investigation, and helps them to answer questions about the meaning and purpose of life, and the nature and consequences of death.

There will be no opportunity here to consider the implications of this theme in its interfaith setting, or to explore the secular varieties of the idea of hope.[3] Nor will it be possible to embrace the question of future survival as it relates to forms of life other than the human; although it is true to say that in biblical thought *all* creation shares in the praises of God.[4] Similarly, the contemporary discussion of eschatology in its wider context, present in the seminal work of such scholars as Jürgen Moltmann[5] and Wolfhart Pannenberg,[6] cannot receive detailed attention at the moment. We shall concentrate rather on the theology of hope in its Christian and biblical perspective, and think first of the eschatological character of hope as a balance, as a tension between the present and the future.

Christian hope is based on a confidence that God has revealed himself, finally and fully, in the Word made flesh (John 1:14). This disclosure becomes the means by which God's salvific purposes for his creation, through judgment, may be achieved (Rev. 21–22). The New Testament

---

[3] For a consideration of hope in its secular manifestations see the study by H. Schwarz, *Eschatology* (Grand Rapids/Cambridge: Eerdmans, 2000), 173–243.

[4] Cf. Ps. 69:34; 148:7–13; Rev. 4:11; 5:13, et al.

[5] J. Moltmann, *Theology of Hope: On the Ground and the Implications of a Christian Eschatology* (New York: Harper & Row, 1967).

[6] W. Pannenberg, *Systematic Theology* (3 vols.; Grand Rapids: Eerdmans, 1991–98). For the work of both Moltmann and Pannenberg see Schwarz, *Eschatology*, 143–51; also R. Bauckham (ed.), *God Will Be All in All: The Eschatology of Jürgen Moltmann* (Edinburgh: T&T Clark, 1999); M. Gilbertson, *God and History in the Book of Revelation: New Testament Studies in Dialogue with Pannenberg and Moltmann* (SNTSMS 124; Cambridge/New York: Cambridge University Press, 2003).

makes it plain that, as a result, the centre of salvation history lies in the Christ-event, which has taken place already; so that in Christ, to use Oscar Cullmann's phrase, time is 'divided anew'.[7] Thereafter, the Christian church awaits the future and decisive parousia of Jesus the Messiah; but, at the same time, it looks back to the moment when history was invaded by that which is supra-historical: in the life and death and exaltation of Jesus the Lord. So the ends of the ages are overlapping us in the present (1 Cor. 10:11), and there is a tension between the hour that is coming, and is now here (John 5:27).[8]

Such an eschatological perspective is relevant to the doctrine of hope. It means that believers may look forward to participating in God's eternal life at the end, but also begin to share it in the present. Christ promises his gifts of the bread and water of life, indeed life itself, now,[9] and not only in the future.[10] By trusting him, it is possible to be reconciled to God and experience his healing, and also to hope for salvation in the new creation.[11] In biblical theology, hope is triple-tensed: it is past, present and future.

This does not affect the truth that Christian hope is *mostly* forward-looking. The saints can rejoice in God's saving activity in ages past; but they are not encouraged to maintain a retrospective outlook on life. Salvation is to be worked out dynamically, in the present and in the light of the future.[12] Believers are called, like St Paul himself, to strain forward to what lies ahead, and press on toward the

---

[7] O. Cullmann, *Christ and Time: The Primitive Christian Conception of Time and History* (London: SCM Press, 1951), esp. 81–93.

[8] See further S.S. Smalley, *John: Evangelist and Interpreter* (2nd edn.; Carlisle: Paternoster Press, 1998), 265–70.

[9] John 6:35; 11:25.

[10] Rev. 7:16; 21:6; 22:17.

[11] Rom. 5:1–11; 8:24–25; Rev. 21:1–4.

[12] Phil. 2:12.

goal for the prize of the upward call of God in Christ Jesus.[13]

The doctrine of the church is germane to this discussion. God's people do not just sit around and hope. They recall his visitation in Christ, and anticipate the final revelation of his glory. Situated between memory and hope, they are allowed to share proleptically in the new age ahead.[14] The church on earth is thus a reminder of God's future, and of the heavenly city to come. John's teaching about the church in Revelation, I would argue, is strongly corporate;[15] and his vision of the new Jerusalem in the Apocalypse[16] relates precisely to the intimate and covenant relationship that God's people will enjoy with him in eternity. But meanwhile, in life and liturgy, in the Lord's Prayer and the Lord's Supper, the Christian community understands itself as the symbol of a future that has already begun.[17] The church maintains a hope that is for ever.

Life after Death

The topic of Christian hope relates directly to the New Testament view of death, which is a factor in God's creation, and belongs to the fundamental order of our world. Death demonstrates our creatureliness, our distance from God and dependence on him. He alone has immortality (1 Tim. 6:16), while everyone and everything else is subject to

---

[13] Phil. 3:13–14. Cf. U. Schnelle, *The History and Theology of the New Testament Writings* (London: SCM Press, 1998), 141–42.

[14] Schwarz, *Eschatology* 370. See also ibid., 370–87.

[15] See S.S. Smalley, 'The Johannine Community and the Letters of John' in M. Bockmuehl and M.B. Thompson (eds.), *A Vision for the Church: Studies in Early Christian Eschatology in Honour of J.P.M. Sweet* (Edinburgh: T&T Clark, 1997), 95–104, esp. 98–99.

[16] Rev. 21:2 – 22:5.

[17] Cf. Schwarz, *Eschatology*, 371–73.

death and decay (1 Cor. 15:45). Moreover, since human existence is eschatological, and we are all on our way to the end, death gives to each moment of our life its singularity.[18]

The Christian view of death is distinctive. In the teaching of the Old Testament there is very little idea of life after death, and almost none of resurrection. There, death is mostly understood as an area of unconsciousness, of suspended animation. Sheol, the realm of departed spirits, is essentially a place where nothing happens; it is a land of forgetfulness in which the shades do not rise up to praise God.[19] According to the New Testament, on the other hand, the Christian perception is that through Christ death can become the means of resurrection and eternal life, and need not be death at all.

Eternal Life

Eternal life is a *gift*. It is the life of God himself, given to believers through Jesus Christ. 'God was in Christ,' as Paul says, 'reconciling the world to himself' (2 Cor. 5:19, NJB). This means that Jesus is the human face of God, and that to see the Son is to see the Father.[20] The theme of 'giving' is important in the context of divine life. God's love for the world was such that he *gave* his only Son, in order that believers could receive eternal life.[21] Similarly, Jesus, who was given virtually nothing throughout his ministry, apart from occasional hospitality and a box of ointment, *gave*

---

[18] Schwarz, *Eschatology*, 257.
[19] Ps. 88:10–12; cf. 90:10. For hope beyond death, in both biblical and post-biblical Judaism, see further N.T. Wright, *The Resurrection of the Son of God* (Christian Origins and the Question of God, vol. 3; London: SPCK, 2003), 85–206.
[20] John 14:9.
[21] John 3:16–17.

himself totally to others. He came not to be served, but to serve. This self-giving reached its climax when Christ gave his life for the world. Through his death, as the perfect offering for human imperfection, and by means of his resurrection, Jesus made it possible for anyone at any time to receive his life, and to be born afresh to a new and living hope.[22]

In his death and exaltation, therefore, Christ became the mediator to humanity of God's forgiveness, and of his eternal life: which is a characteristically Johannine description of 'salvation'. In the Christian scheme Jesus is the unique way to God, through whom alone believers can understand God's truth and receive his life.[23] This gift of eternal life is best understood in terms of a relationship between God and his people. It implies an alliance that is living and growing, and a knowledge of God which involves the mind but is ultimately personal, and beyond human reason. In the saying of Jesus, 'this is eternal life ... to know you, the only true God, and Jesus Christ whom you have sent' (John 17:3).[24]

Eternal life is also, secondly, a *quality*. Christian life is eternal because God gives it, and he is both sovereign and eternal. But this life is qualitative, and not quantitative. God's world and our own are clearly related, since he is the Creator and Saviour of the universe; and, among the New Testament writers, it is the authors of the Johannine corpus

---

[22]   Mark 10:45; Gal. 1:4; Heb. 10:11–12; 1 Pet. 1:3.

[23]   John 3:15; 14:6. Cf. J.A.T. Robinson, 'What Future for a Unique Christ?' in *Where Three Ways Meet: Last Essays and Sermons* (London: SCM Press, 1987), 9–17; also B. Hebblethwaite, 'The Impossibility of Multiple Incarnations', *Theology* 104 (2001), 323–34.

[24]   See further the Doctrine Commission Report, *The Mystery of Salvation: The Story of God's Gift. A Report by the Doctrine Commission of the General Synod of the Church of England* (London: Church House Publishing, 1995), 120–43 (on 'Receiving the Gift').

who describe that connection most sensitively.[25] Neverthe-less, heaven and earth ultimately belong to different planes; for one is spiritual and eternal, while the other is material and temporal. As a result, the life of eternity cannot be measured.

Everything conspires to make us think otherwise, since belonging to this world inevitably involves using temporal categories with which to describe and determine natural life, and we are instinctively inclined to apply such delimitations to spiritual existence. Prayers which end, 'for ever and ever, Amen', and liturgical references to the Eucharist as the 'food and drink' of eternal life, provide us with an encouragement to think of eternity as an endless succession of 'years', and of the sacrament as a feast which lasts for an inordinate length of time.

The imagery of John's Revelation appears to move in the same direction, and to suggest that it is possible to measure eternity in terms of time and space. But when the prophet-seer speaks of silence occurring in heaven for about half an hour (Rev. 8:1), or of Satan being bound for one thousand years (Rev. 20:2), and when the heavenly city is measured by the angel in miles and cubits (Rev. 21:15–17), the language and ideas of time and space are obviously being employed, in a typically Hebrew-Christian literary manner, to represent the truths of eternity. For the life which God gives is to be enjoyed, and cannot be 'measured'. In the divine plane time does not exist, since 'with the Lord one day is like a thousand years, and a thousand years are like one day' (2 Pet. 3:8). What matters, then, is not the *extent* of the eternal life that is experienced by the church, but its *quality*.

---

[25] See S.S. Smalley, *Thunder and Love: John's Revelation and John's Community* (Milton Keynes: Nelson Word, 1994), 147–57.

Eternal life, on the Christian showing, is a gift and a quality. Thirdly, it is a *progression*. We have touched already on the implications of New Testament eschatology for the subject of hope. To become a Christian while on earth is to share already in the dimension of eternity. Receiving the gift of eternal life is to enter God's family, become new people and begin to live a new life.[26] For the saints, the life of eternity is a present reality, as well as a future hope. Members of God's church, therefore, live in two 'worlds' at once; and this means that they are not permitted to escape the demands of justice and love in this world, by anticipating the rewards of the next. On the contrary, we are all called until we die to live as Christian citizens who have a responsibility towards the society surrounding us.

Such theology, which affirms the importance of the material, as well as spiritual, dimension, is illuminated in the New Testament by the teaching in the Johannine literature about what I like to term the 'sacramental'. Both the Apocalypse and John's Gospel are rich in their use of symbols, which bring together the levels of matter and spirit. The fourth evangelist, for example, perceives that, with the tabernacling of the Word of God among his creatures, a final intersection of earth and heaven has taken place.[27] In the seven dominical 'signs' of John's Gospel, as a result, ordinary facts such as water, wine, bread, sight and physical life itself, *become* what they represent; Jesus not only multiplies loaves, for instance, he also provides spiritual sustenance in the Christian life.[28] John's symbolism has moved on into a characteristic sacramentalism, whereby – like the Word himself – the earthly becomes the carrier of the heavenly.[29]

---

[26] Rom. 6:4, 23; 8:15–16; 2 Cor. 5:17.
[27] John 1:14; 1:51.
[28] John 6:25–40.
[29] See further Smalley, *John*, 232–38.

The same is manifestly true of Revelation. As with any part of the drama of the Apocalypse, John's symbolism must be read from the perspective of both dimensions, physical and spiritual, temporal and eternal. So the seven angels are commanded from the *heavenly* tent to pour out their bowls of wrath upon the *earth*.[30] Similarly, the apparently material elements of thunder and fire, of water and light, and the earthly instruments of sickle and sword, of thrones and incense, have a double, spiritual significance, both judgmental and salvific, to which in each case they point. Like the fourth evangelist after him, accordingly, John the Divine does not stop with the symbolic; he introduces a truly sacramental focus to his thought and theology. The concept of human salvation through divine discrimination is not only pictured, but also made real. The destruction of Babylon (Rev. 17 – 18), for example, is not simply an evocation of God's wrath in response to human rebellion; it also shows what actually happens in society whenever systemic evil and idolatrous falsehood prevail. The light which shines eternally in the new Jerusalem, through the glory of God and in response to faith (Rev. 21:23–24), also and tangibly breaks through the darkness of this world now.[31]

This intersection, between earth and heaven and time as well as eternity, relates to the concept of life with God in Christ. Believers, who through faith possess eternal life, do not die spiritually. Unless the end of the world comes first, they die physically, but remain alive spiritually for ever. In that case, God's eternal life is shared both before and after death; and this is a continuation, a progression, of the *same* relationship. There is no *dis*continuity, nor is a completely

---

[30] Rev. 15:5 – 16:1

[31] Cf. S.S. Smalley, *The Revelation to John: A Commentary on the Greek Text of the Apocalypse* (London: SPCK, 2005), 13–15; see also Smalley, *Thunder and Love*, 177–78.

fresh existential encounter established. All that happens after death is that the barriers of time and space are removed, and it becomes possible to see God face to face, and share fully in his eternal life.[32] Such an understanding impinges on John's presentation in the Apocalypse of heaven as a 'new creation' (Rev. 21:1), and we shall consider that imagery later.

It is important, meanwhile, to examine the basis for this eternal hope. In the Christian scheme, the certainty of God's gift of life, both here and hereafter, rests on what the New Testament has to say about the resurrection of Christ and of the Christian; and to that teaching we now turn.

Resurrection

The witness of the New Testament, apart from the Gospels, provides a clear affirmation that the hope of eternal life, before and after death, depends on God's salvific work in Christ. Because he died and rose again, we too can triumph through him.[33] But that testimony to the significance of the resurrection is mostly Paul's, even if it finds echoes elsewhere in New Testament literature, notably in the Easter summaries of Acts, and in parts of Revelation.[34] Moreover, the hermeneutical character of the tradition concerning the resurrection of Jesus appears to be the result of primitive theological reflection, rather than belonging to the resurrection narratives themselves, as these are found especially in the Gospels of Matthew, Luke and John. If such a thesis may be sustained, as we shall see,

---

[32]   1 John 3:2; Rev. 21:1–7.
[33]   Rom. 4:24–25; 6:5.
[34]   See Acts 2:22–24, 31–33, 36; 3:13–15, 26; 4:10–12; 5:30–32; 10:37–43; 13:28–39; Rev. 1:5, 17–18; 2:8. Note also 1 Pet. 1:3–5, probably 1 John 1:1, and possibly Heb. 11:19.

it has implications for the historicity of those Gospel accounts.

So what about the resurrection of Jesus? This is not the place to attempt a major discussion of this key issue, which has recently received comprehensive treatment in the magisterial study by Tom Wright, the present Bishop of Durham, *The Resurrection of the Son of God* (2003).[35] I shall assume that it is not necessary to give credence to the well known and sceptical views attracted by this topic, since these are largely subjective, and unsupported by worthy textual and traditional evidence. I refer, for example, to the suggestion that the whole idea rests on an illusion, since Jesus did not really die, but revived after being in a coma for some hours; or that his body was cleverly removed from the tomb by his enemies or friends; or that the notion of God raising Jesus from the dead was a mental delusion on the part of the disciples, who longed for the Lord's continued existence in their lives.

Each of those three theories depends on the involvement of the disciples in an unlikely deception; unless it be argued that those hostile to Jesus stole his body, although evidently the Jewish authorities did all they could to prevent this from happening (Matt. 27:62–66). So far as the followers of Jesus were concerned, it taxes credibility to suppose that they would base their mission – and even risk their lives – on the basis of a palpable fraud. It is true that, when we speak of the resurrection of Christ, we pass beyond what is capable of historical description and analysis, into a realm that demands faith as well as reason.[36] But this need not deter us from looking once more

---

[35] See note 19.

[36] Cf. E.C. Hoskyns and F.N. Davey, *Crucifixion-Resurrection: The Pattern of the Theology and Ethics of the New Testament* (ed. G.S. Wakefield; London: SPCK, 1981), 279–92, esp. 280.

at the biblical evidence itself, in order to assess its reliability.[37]

The resurrection narratives in the Gospels agree in their basic substance, but not in their detail; and this by itself suggests independent, authentic witness, rather than collusion. For example, it is not clear whether Jesus appeared to his disciples in Galilee (as Mark implies), or Jerusalem (Luke), or both (Matthew and John). Furthermore, the number of women who went to the sepulchre differs in each account: one in John, two in Matthew, three in Mark and more than three in Luke. Again, the 'messenger' figures associated with the tomb vary according to all four evangelists: one young man (Mark), two men (Luke), an angel from heaven (Matthew), and two angels (John). Apart from these minor disagreements, there are four features in the narratives themselves pointing to their primitive origin:

1. The evangelists tell the story of Jesus up to his resurrection with increasing reference to the Old Testament, and the way in which, through him, prophecy was being fulfilled. Even the post-crucifixion and burial narratives, particularly in the Fourth Gospel, include biblical resonances.[38] But the Gospel accounts of the resurrection are noticeably devoid of scriptural quotation or allusion, and give the impression that they are dramatic and breathless, personal stories, rather than the result of biblical and theological reflection. This lack of embroidery is all the more remarkable in view of the fact that what is evidently the earliest form of the Christian kerygma, quoted by Paul at 1 Corinthians 15:1–5, explicitly states that

[37] For the following section see Wright, *Resurrection of the Son*, 587–615.
[38] E.g. John 19:36–37, 39.

Christ was raised on the third day 'in accordance with the scriptures' (v. 4). The preaching of Peter in Acts 2 and elsewhere elaborates the connection between Hebrew prophecy and the resurrection of God's Messiah. But, although they had the materials to hand, the evangelists do not.

2. A second feature to notice in the Gospel records of the Easter event is the nature of the resurrection body of Jesus. The New Testament accounts of the resurrection agree that it involved not simply the revival of a corpse, but a new form of spiritual existence. However, the representation of its nature differs. Paul says that when Christ was raised from the dead, he was given a new 'body of glory', by which he was able to reveal himself directly to his earthly followers (Phil. 3:21, q.v.). The evangelists, on the other hand, seem concerned to underscore the material character of Jesus' appearance after the resurrection. Even if he is sometimes unrecognised, vanishes in the course of a meal at Emmaus, comes and goes through locked doors, and finally ascends into heaven, the risen Jesus also walks and talks with his disciples, eats with them and is touched by them.[39] This restraint is remarkable. Had the Easter stories in the Gospels been invented on the basis of Daniel 12:2–3, the most familiar Jewish 'resurrection' text, the Gospel writers would almost certainly have portrayed the risen Jesus as 'shining like a bright and eternal star' (v. 3). Among the evangelists, it is only the appearance of angelic figures that is said to be dazzling.[40] The post-resurrection portrait of Jesus accordingly suggests that it rests on very

---

[39] See John 20:14; Luke 24:31; John 20:19; Luke 24:51; Luke 24:13–30; Matt. 28:9; John 20:27.
[40] Matt. 28:3; Luke 24:4.

early, authentic, and in many ways surprising, memories.[41]

3. A third element to be noted in the resurrection narratives, according to the New Testament Gospels, is the prominent part played by women. The evangelists agree with Paul that Jesus appeared only to a limited circle of people, although Paul does record a mass disclosure to more than five hundred people at once (1 Cor. 15:6). But in all four Gospels it is women who are the first to know and report that the tomb of Jesus on the first Easter morning was empty.[42] The men arrive at the scene later. In the Mediterranean world of the first century AD, women were not regarded as credible witnesses.[43] No doubt for this reason they are screened out of the primitive version of the Christian gospel at 1 Corinthians 15:4–8, where Paul says that Jesus appeared to Peter, the Twelve and to James, the brother of the Lord (15:7), although James is not mentioned in the Gospel accounts of the resurrection. The fact that all four evangelists later include women as crucial witnesses to the empty tomb, and in differing ways, suggests not only that they were present in the first place, but also that their testimony was in due course discovered to be true.[44]

4. Finally, it is striking that the resurrection narratives in the Gospels do not even hint at, let alone include, the promise of future hope for believers. Elsewhere in the New Testament the resurrection of Christ is understood as the basis for the resurrection of

[41] Cf. G. Gloege, *The Day of His Coming: The Man in the Gospels* (London: SCM Press, 1963), 281.
[42] Mark 16:1–7; Matt. 28:1–8; Luke 24:1–10; John 20:1–2.
[43] Cf. Josephus, *Ant.* 4. 219 ('From women let no evidence be accepted, because of the levity and temerity of their sex').
[44] See further Wright, *Resurrection of the Son*, 607–608.

Christians.[45] The emphasis in the Gospels is more basic, and the stories lack theological elaboration. Although they were written after a period in which the early church had been able to reflect on the implications of the Easter event, the accounts of the evangelists are not concerned with life after death, or the bodily resurrection of Christians, but with the challenge presented to the followers of the risen Christ to witness to him in the present. This is very clear in Luke (24:46–49), Matthew (28:19–20) and John (21:11, 15–22); but even in Mark (16:6–7) the women are given a task which points in the direction of a mission to be completed.[46] Such direct reporting implies personal recollections of what happened on the third day, derived from an impressively primitive and originally oral tradition.

This brief survey of the resurrection narratives in the four Gospels seems to demand the conclusion that the accounts by the evangelists rest on evidence that chronologically *precedes* the formulation of the Easter message elsewhere in the New Testament. It may not be possible, on this basis, to claim unequivocally that the Easter event itself, and these early testimonies to its occurrence, are to be regarded as 'historical'. However, I am prepared to argue that such witness provides a reasonable basis on which to affirm the resurrection of Christ, and the eternal hope of the church to which the New Testament as a whole makes reference. It is also very significant, in my view, that the sepulchre of Jesus evidently remained empty, and that his body was never produced. Easter faith includes much more than an empty tomb, but that piece of evidence is a crucial part of it. Moreover, it is a clear fact of history that, on the basis of

---

45 Rom. 6:4–5; 1 Cor. 15:20–21; 1 Pet. 1:3, et al.
46 Wright, *Resurrection of the Son*, 629–31.

post-crucifixion experience, the followers of Jesus began a lasting testimony to his presence on earth through the Spirit. The Christian church came into being, and still exists.

We may conclude that when the early church took over from biblical and post-biblical Judaism the unusual idea of resurrection,[47] and developed it with reference to Christ, the Christian and their relationship, its members did so as a result not of subjective imagination or delusion, but on the basis of testimony to an historical process. To this extent it is possible to speak of the truth of the resurrection, giving to believers in all ages the grounds for a living hope that is for ever.

What Kind of Body?

We shall return in due course to the further implications of Christ's resurrection for the life of believers after death. Meanwhile, there is an intriguing question that may be asked at this point. With Paul, we need to enquire about the *nature* of the resurrection body of Christians. 'How are the dead raised? With what kind of body do they come?' (1 Cor. 15:35). The *timing* for the adoption of that body will also be the subject of a later enquiry.

The New Testament suggests that, following the raising of Christ from the dead, Christian believers share in three resurrections: by faith at baptism (Rom. 6:4), at death (Rev. 20:5–6), and at the end (1 Cor. 15:51–52). Resurrection to new life on earth does not, perhaps, present us with too much difficulty, since it is a spiritual rather than a physical phenomenon. But the concept of resurrection at death, or after it, is potentially more problematic. A good model for

---

[47] See *1 Enoch* 51:1–5; 58:1–6; *Adam and Eve (Apoc)* 37:1–6, et al.

understanding this notion is the resurrection body of Jesus himself; for, as we have seen, the fact that the Father raised him from the dead has become the means of humanity's resurrection.[48] The Easter accounts in the Gospels make it clear that, after the resurrection, Jesus was not a disembodied spirit. Indeed, he denies this possibility explicitly: 'a ghost does not have flesh and bones as you see that I have' (Luke 24:39). The risen Christ was in the end easily identifiable, and could be seen and touched.[49] He was the same person, who was known to the disciples during his earthly ministry. Yet there was a difference, for while still on earth and until he ascended to the Father he was participating fully in the dimension of eternity. That is why he could act in a way that was supernatural, as well as natural.

This parallel has limited value, since while believers are called to be *like* Christ in time, and are promised that they will resemble him in heaven,[50] Christians are not Christ. Nevertheless, the model is helpful in two directions. First, it points to the truth that life after death involves change, as well as continuity. Eternity is not simply an extension of this world, but without any of its difficulties. The holy city of Revelation 21 – 22 speaks of a covenant relationship between God and his people that is new, as well as spiritual and enduring. This alliance will demonstrate connections with positive aspects of time and space; but, in the course of it, the saints will also know the Father afresh, because now they see him face to face. Secondly, the resurrection body of Jesus suggests that the form to be assumed by his followers after death will be identifiable. As Paul says, on earth they have a 'physical body', but in heaven a 'spiritual' counterpart (1 Cor. 15:44). Physical features

---

[48] Cf. Acts 3:8–12, et al.
[49] Cf. 1 John 1:1–3.
[50] See 1 Pet. 2:21; 1 John 3:2.

disappear after death, but the individual personality remains in its different, spiritual expression.

There will be more to say about this topic in due course. Meanwhile, I should like to give some brief attention to the idea of reincarnation, since it is germane to the theology of life after death.

Reincarnation

It is probably true to say that the longing for continued existence beyond death, in the case of oneself or others, is instinctively human. Admittedly, in the ancient world, epic poets such as Homer found no place for resurrection of any kind.[51] But there was in fact a common belief, held by early philosophers, according to which the dead returned to some type of bodily existence. This was the theory of *metempsychosis*, the transmigration or reincarnation of souls, which Celsus, in the second century AD, regarded as the basis for the Christian doctrine of resurrection.[52] Moreover, forms of reincarnation belong, as I know from experience, to systems of African religion right down to this day; in such schemes the spirit of a departed person comes back to earth, at some stage, to take up residence in someone else, often a member of the same family.[53] Thought of this kind certainly indicates faith in survival after death, but it remains to be seen whether it is in line with the teaching of the New Testament about eternal life. Three points may be made in this connection:

---

[51]   Cf. Homer, *Iliad* 24.549–51; 24.756.

[52]   So Origen, *Con.Cels.* 7.32. See further Wright, *Resurrection of the Son*, 32–84, esp. 77–79.

[53]   See N.Q. King, *Religions of Africa: A Pilgrimage Into Traditional Religions* (New York and London: Harper & Row, 1970), 62–82, esp. 77–82; also E.B. Idowu, *African Traditional Religion: A Definition* (London: SCM Press, 1973), 187–89.

1. There is no biblical evidence for the idea of reincarnation. There is some witness to post-mortem survival in the Old Testament, and abundant testimony to resurrection through Christ in the New Testament. But this is radically different from the notion of reincarnation. In 1 Samuel 28 there is an account of Saul's visit to the medium at Endor, as a result of which the prophet Samuel is 'brought up' out of the ground from the dead.[54] However, this episode grazes the edge of necromancy, and manifestly cannot be regarded as a classic example of reincarnation.

2. If the discussion so far about eternal life, and the hope of personal resurrection, may be accepted as valid, it is very difficult to build theories of reincarnation into such theology. Indeed, the one must exclude the other. Communities are important in the social context of Christianity, and the ecclesiological dimensions of the gospel should never be overlooked. On the other hand, while there is no place here for individualism, the significance of the individual must also be affirmed.[55] God did not create, and Christ did not redeem, anonymous masses of humanity, but individual people with separate and distinctive personalities. According to biblical teaching, it is within God's purpose that each of these individuals, created with the intention of being made in the image of God, should be rescued from the powers of evil and brought into fellowship with him through Jesus Christ.[56] The earthly ministry of Jesus himself clearly included an involvement with separate characters, and this may be regarded as a token of the divine concern for individuals in eternity, as well as in time.

---

[54] 1 Sam. 28:3–25, esp. vv. 13–14.
[55] Cf. Smalley, 'Johannine Community', 102–104.
[56] Gen. 1:26–27; Rom. 8:28–30; 1 Cor. 15:49; 2 Cor. 3:18; Col. 3:10.

3. The eschatology of the New Testament is linear and teleological in character, whereas the notion of reincarnation demands a cyclical view of existence which is Hellenistic, rather than Judaeo-Christian.[57] In this case, it is not easy to understand how theories of reincarnation can fit together with Christian belief in a recognisable resurrection *body*. If reincarnation takes place in a circular fashion, what happens to the 'spirits', which are included in this process, at the consummation? To whom do they belong, and whose resurrection body, if any, do they assume?

On the Christian showing, resurrection evidently makes more sense than reincarnation. Positively, the gospel of the Lord speaks of life in Christ, for individual believers and for the church, in this world and in the next. Jesus is the resurrection, and because of this he is eternal life, and the answer to death.[58] Just here is the basis and centre of a Christian hope that is everlasting.[59]

---

[57] See Schwarz, *Eschatology*, 97–103.
[58] John 11:25; 14:6.
[59] For the material in this chapter see further Cullmann, *Christ and Time*, 231–42 (on resurrection faith and hope in relation to redemptive history).

2

Salvation Through Judgment

God's Judgment

The Christian theology of hope must include some consideration of the topic of divine judgment. If believers may be assured that, through the loving work of God in Christ, they are able to receive the gift of eternal life,[1] this implies that such a status is likely to be withheld from those who, for whatever reason, reject the divine offer. The New Testament presents us with a God who, in Jesus the Messiah, has not only revealed himself as Creator and Saviour, but also made plain the nature of good in relation to evil.[2] Since God has been disclosed as a Father whose love and truth and goodness are perfect and complete, as a totally holy being, human failure to meet his moral standards must inevitably both attract his grace, and merit his justice.[3] The theme of the judgment of the dead is an extension of the general concept of divine justice; and, not surprisingly, the belief that in the end God dispenses judgment as well as salvation to his creatures is fundamental to the systems of all the major world religions, as well as to Christianity.[4]

---

[1] Rom. 5:21; 8:11.
[2] Cf. Rev. 15:3–4.
[3] Rom. 3:21–26.
[4] See S.G.F. Brandon, *The Judgment of the Dead: The Idea of Life after Death in the Major Religions* (New York: Scribners, 1967), esp. 98–135.

As we shall see, the Christian scheme does not associate
judgment solely with what happens after death. However,
it is probably true to say that 'judgment' is commonly
equated with God's discrimination, and the terrifying
punishment of the wicked, at the *last* day. Such a picture is
an exaggeration of the theme of divine judgment, stem-
ming from the Middle Ages, and owes much to the paint-
ing and drama of that period. The depiction by
Michelangelo of 'The Last Judgment', on the east wall of
the Sistine Chapel in Rome, for example, follows this tradition. It portrays the scene at the end of the ages, with God
and Christ sitting in judgment, and the righteous being
taken up by the angels into heaven, while the unfaithful
descend, with the encouragement of demons, into the fires
of perpetual torment. A similar icon appears at the apex of
the Mappa Mundi, in Hereford Cathedral; while the
related idea of selling one's soul to the Satan ('sin now, pay
later') belongs to theatrical presentations that include a
Faustian theme.

It is possible to argue that there is biblical precedent for
illustrating the subject of divine judgment in this way, and
that a basis can be found not least from imagery in the
Apocalypse.[5] We will explore some relevant examples of
such symbolism in a moment. Meanwhile, three general
points about the Christian understanding of God's judgmental activity may help to focus our attention on its
essential nature:

1.   There is, to some extent, a correlation between natural
     and divine justice. 'Judgment' on wrongdoing, in
     social terms, is an expected and even welcome phe-
     nomenon. If human beings behave lawlessly, and are
     brought to court and proved guilty, it is not

---

[5]   See Rev. 18:2–23; 19:17 – 20:15, et al.; cf. also Matt. 22:1–14; 24:45–51;
25:14–30.

considered unfair for such people to be sentenced, and punished accordingly. We do not have to be lawyers to know the basic meaning of justice issues, and judgment in the community.

2. However, this model cannot be used without qualification to delineate the judgment of God. The biblical evidence will not allow us to claim, for example, that 'the punishment must fit the crime', or that God's reaction to human sin must always be in proportion to its extent: the larger the sin, the greater the wrath. Divine justice is a reality; however, in this area a living God who cares for individuals, rather than an impersonal system, confronts us.

3. As with all considerations of the Christian view of life and death, and notably in relation to the topic of God's judgment, sensitivity is needed. Early murals of the final judgment, such as the one on the north nave wall in the eleventh-century parish church of St Nicholas Oddington, in Gloucestershire, rarely hesitate to disguise the enjoyment experienced by the saints at the fate of the wicked; indeed, it may be regarded as part of the eternal reward which the faithful are due to inherit. But my point is that, theologically, divine judgment affects us all; so that any investigation of this truth, and the conclusions we draw from it, should always be carried out in love.

Judgment in the Old Testament

The Flood

We are now ready to look at some instances of God's judgment in the Judaeo-Christian scriptures, beginning with the Flood. According to Genesis 6 – 9, the Noachic saga

was the result of human rebellion against God, who 'saw
that the wickedness of people was great in the earth' (6:5).
Yahweh acted in response to an unrighteousness that was
total. Yet his judgment was not separated from his mercy,
so that included in the statement that he had 'decided to
make an end of all flesh' (6:13), was the instruction to Noah
that he should make an ark (v. 14). The very water that was
regarded as an expression of divine judgment became the
means of life for Noah and his family; and in the New Testament (1 Pet. 3:18–22) this salvific pattern is associated
with the waters of baptism.[6] There is also a positive outcome to the story, in that after the Flood God established
an eternal covenant between himself and the whole of creation.[7]

The Exodus

A second example of divine judgment in the Old Testament is to be found in the Exodus of Israel from Egypt, and
the years of wandering in the wilderness brought upon
God's people (summarised in Deut. 1 – 2). The Exodus
itself cannot be regarded as part of God's judgment; but all
that happened to the Egyptians, and much that was experienced by the Israelites during this period, is certainly
understood by the writers of the Pentateuch as the result of
God's judgmental activity. In the face of Israel's constant
and rebellious murmuring, which came to its climax in the
incident of the golden calf described in Exodus 32, Moses
declares that Yahweh is angered both by the people themselves and with Moses on their account.[8] One result of this

---

[6] Cf. also Heb. 11:7; 2 Pet. 2:5; 3:5–9. See E.G. Selwyn, *The First Epistle of St Peter* (London: Macmillan, 1949), 201–206.
[7] Gen. 8:21; 9:8–17. For the problems in this narrative see further R.N. Whybray, 'Genesis', *OBC*, 46–47.
[8] See Deut. 1:34–37.

was the actual length of time spent by the Israelites in the wilderness, and the fact that many of the travellers, including Moses himself, failed to enter the Promised Land (Deut. 34:1–7). But God never forgot his people, according to the Deuteronomist, or the covenant he made with them on Sinai. On the contrary, the Lord used their hardship and adversity to accomplish his own purposes for Israel, and bring its members into their own land (Josh. 1:1–9).

The Exile

A final example of the present theme is to be found in the account of Israel's exile to Babylon in the sixth century BC (Jer. 52). Like the Exodus, the Exile had a profound effect on the national and spiritual life of the Israelites. For instance, the exiles themselves felt that they had been cut off from God, because they were far from the Temple at Jerusalem, and unable to sing the songs of Zion in a foreign land (Ps. 137:4). But this situation provided them with an opportunity to learn more about the presence of God with his people than they had ever known before. Among the Old Testament prophets, it is Ezekiel who says most about the meaning and effect of the Exile. He regards it as God's judgment on the corruption and rebellion of Israel, stretching back to the earliest days of her history. Despite God's holiness and faithfulness, the prophet claims, Israel had broken the covenant and played the spiritual harlot (Ezek. 16:15–22); and, before she can share God's forgiveness and be restored to her own land, she must experience divine judgment (Ezek. 20:36). But that justice will lead in reality to a future hope. Israel, who had known Yahweh in judgment, will be able to stand again in his holy presence, and know him as her own Lord (Ezek. 20:44).

The Meaning of Judgment

These examples raise four major issues that are associated with the theological significance of God's judgment in the Old Testament:

1. First, divine justice is related to the concept of *holiness*. Because God's being and nature are complete, his holiness inevitably clashes with human ungodliness. If we choose to be less than good and loving and just, God can only respond by putting into our consciences his standards of goodness and love and justice. Such a reaction relates to the biblical category of 'wrath', which will be considered more fully later. It also impinges on the notion of cultic holiness in Judaism,[9] and on the desire for ritual and personal holiness in the Qumran community.[10]

2. Secondly, the Old Testament seems to suggest at times that human *suffering* is the result of divine judgment. For example, the proud rebellion of Dathan and Abiram against the leadership of Moses is said, by the writer of Numbers, to have provoked an earthquake that swallowed them up (Num. 16:27–33); because 14,700 Israelites complained that Moses and Aaron had in this way destroyed God's people, they were in turn killed by a plague (Num. 16:41–49); and when Uzzah tried to steady the ark of the covenant on its way to Jerusalem, he was struck by God's anger (2 Sam. 6:6–7). In such instances, it appears that God the Judge is directing the fate of individuals, nations, and indeed humanity as a whole. However, the Old

---

[9] Cf. Exod. 26:33; Lev. 11:44; Num. 15:40, et al.

[10] So 1QM 14:12; 1QS 8:21; 1QH 11.12, et al. For the idea of holiness in the Old Testament see further H. Seebass, 'Holy', *NIDNTT* 2 (1976), 223–28, esp. 226–28.

Testament writers themselves, who saw the hand of God in every event, probably made the connection between human error and the exercise of divine justice.[11] This interpretation follows a syllogism, as in the case of Sodom: the impurity of the inhabitants of Sodom and Gomorrah was common knowledge; their cities were destroyed by fire; therefore God had punished them (Gen. 18–19).[12] This is not to say that God cannot intervene in this way, or that natural disasters cannot bring people back to him. But, as the poem of Job makes clear, the presence of pain in the world should never be regarded automatically as the responsibility of a God who is judgmental. God does not cause suffering, even if he may use it.

3. Thirdly, the biblical view of divine judgment is *positive*. It is necessary to balance the Old Testament representation of God's justice with the teaching of Jesus and of the New Testament writers. God's judgment must accord with his nature, and he has disclosed himself not only as Judge, but also as the merciful Father of our Lord Jesus Christ; he dispenses life as well as justice, and both derive from his love.[13] Corrective judgment may be a necessary part of God's fatherly nature, given that he is loving and holy. He may well, on occasions, discipline us 'for our good, in order that we may share his holiness' (Heb. 12:10).[14]

---

[11] Within and beyond Judaism, however, the responsibility for suffering was transferred from God to the Satan, and human tribulation itself becomes a proof of goodness, rather than wickedness. Cf. e.g. *Adam and Eve (Vita)* 9:1 – 11:3; *(Apoc)* 17:1 – 19:3; *Asc. Isa.* 2:1–5; also the teaching of Jesus in such a passage as Matt. 5:1–12 par. Note in addition the victorious significance of Christian martyrdom (Rev. 2:13; 6:9–11; Ignatius, *Rom.* 6:1 – 7:3, et al.).

[12] See esp. Gen. 19:24–29.

[13] Cf. Ps. 76:8–9; Lam. 3:32–33; also John 3:14–19; 1 Pet. 1:3–9.

[14] See the whole passage, Heb. 12:7–11.

But if God's being is understood solely as judgmental, and not also as salvific, there is a danger of representing him in the end as *unjust*, rather than just. This makes nonsense of the message of prophets like Amos, who appealed for human justice precisely on the grounds of the just character of God.[15] According to Amos, moreover, God's judgment leads to the hope of Israel's restoration.[16] A similar pattern of salvation *through* restorative, and not retributive, judgment belongs also to the three Old Testament examples of divine justice we considered earlier. The waters of the Flood were the means of Noah's safety; the Exodus sufferings belonged to God's plan for Israel's future; and the Exile led on to the Return.

4. A final issue, which warrants some consideration in this context, is that of judgment in relation to *the living and the dead*. The writers of the Old Testament mostly regarded God's judgment as present, and to be experienced during this life on earth. In the words attributed to God by the author of Deuteronomy (32:35),

> vengeance is mine, and recompense,
> for the time when their foot shall slip;
> because the day of their calamity is at hand,
> their doom comes swiftly.[17]

It is interesting, incidentally, that this note of discrimination is followed almost immediately by the promise of God's vindication in compassion (v. 36). There is no clear reference yet, then, to divine judgment being exercised after death, except possibly at Daniel 12:2.[18]

---

[15] Amos 5:14–24, esp. v. 24.
[16] Amos 9:9–15.
[17] Cf. Schwarz, *Eschatology*, 41.
[18] See also the uncertain texts at Job 19:25–27 and Isa. 25:8 (26:19).

On the other hand, as the Old Testament period progressed, and Israel suffered increasing oppression, the idea developed (particularly in apocalyptic literature) that God would step into history and rescue his people.[19] That great 'Day of the Lord', ushered in by an earthly Messiah or a heavenly Son of man, was to be above all a day of judgment, when the enemies of God would be doomed and the righteous vindicated (see notably Zech. 9 and Dan. 7). By the time of Jesus the Messiah, such an expectation and hope had grown into the belief, present in the intertestamental literature,[20] that the coming judgment would involve everyone, both living and dead. Such is the background to the concept of divine judgment in much of the New Testament; and to this we now turn.

Judgment in the New Testament

Both John the Baptist and Jesus spoke of the dawning of God's kingdom, and claimed that its imminence demanded human repentance.[21] But there is an obvious difference in the two proclamations. John was the forerunner of the Messiah (Mark 1:2–8), whereas Jesus was identified as the Son of God, and the Christ himself (Mark 1:11; 8:29). In other words, the arrival of Jesus on the scene produced a crisis. He brought to the world in a new way the rule of God, and inaugurated its establishment in society and among individuals. As a result, people are now required to make room for the arrival of the sovereign Judge and King in the person of his Son.[22] They need to be

---

[19] See further Smalley, *Thunder and Love*, 24–26.
[20] Cf. *1 Enoch* 102:1 – 103:15, et al.
[21] Cf. Matt. 3:2; Mark 1:15.
[22] Cf. Rev. 19:1–8.

like servants awaiting the return of their master, or brides-maids anticipating the arrival of the bridegroom.[23] Moral actions on the part of humanity in the present will have future consequences; and Jesus represented this as 'the day of judgment', when account is to be rendered even for every careless word uttered.[24] Acknowledgement of Jesus on earth leads accordingly to vindication before the Father in heaven, whereas denial now results in rejection later.[25]

This future judgmental 'Day' appears to resemble the pattern of discrimination, in the Old Testament and intertestamental period, which we have already noted. After a period of suffering and disaster, the Son of man will appear in glory and the end will arrive.[26] At that point, all nations will stand before the King to be judged in the light of what they have done or failed to do; then the righteous will go away to eternal life, while the rest will depart into eternal punishment.[27] But there is an important difference. Judgment now takes place in the light of human reaction to Jesus Christ. The divine standards that have been manifested most clearly in him are those which now apply, and it is these that provide the markers for testing the faith and conduct of the world's inhabitants. Since the Word became flesh, God's kingdom has arrived in a way previously unknown; and judgment of any kind, present or future, now takes place through him.[28]

23 Luke 12:35–40; Matt. 25:1–13.
24 Matt. 12:36.
25 Matt. 10:32–33.
26 Luke 21:25–28.
27 Matt. 25:31–46; cf. Rev. 20:11–15.
28 John 1:14; 3:18; 5:22.

Judgment and God's Nature

Divine justice and human error

We have seen that there is a difference between the idea of judgment presented by the writers of the Old Testament, and the same notion as it occurs in the New Testament; and the difference is made by the advent of Jesus himself. There is a further variation. The literature of the Old Testament, as we have already noticed, sometimes implies that death and disaster are evidence of God's justice, particularly if the rules of the Law have been disobeyed. This outlook became less pronounced as time went on; and the later prophets of Israel were in any case concerned to teach that faithfulness to God is preferable to idolatry, and that right conduct is more important than the external observance of rules.[29] When the early Christians thought of divine judgment, similarly, they regarded its motivation as God's reaction to the unholy nature of human beings, rather than as a failure to act in accordance with moral legislation.[30]

Ananias and Sapphira

Nevertheless, occasional incidents in the New Testament apparently follow an Old Testament model, and suggest that death and disaster may follow a wrong action as the direct result of God's judgment. A famous example is to be found in the story of Ananias and Sapphira, who both fell dead as soon as they lied to Peter about the value of their property, which they were pretending to give in full to the Christian community (Acts 5:1–11). As in the Old Testament examples we have considered, the deaths of Ananias

---

[29] Jer. 2:1–13; Mic. 6:8, et al.
[30] Cf. Rom. 1:18–32; 2 Tim. 3:1 – 4:1.

and his wife were evidently *construed* by the writer of Acts as a moment of judgment. It may be presumed, however, that the immediate cause of death on the part of both victims was shock; in the case of Sapphira, this was doubled by the discovery of her husband's death. We are not compelled to deny that the hand of God was in this event, although it is probably more balanced and appropriate to say that the couple brought their own judgment on themselves, rather than that God 'struck them dead'. On the other side, God's intervention can certainly be seen in the *results* of this incident, most of which were extremely beneficial to the church (vv. 11–16).[31]

God's nature and standards

This discussion brings into focus the *nature* of God himself, and three summary points may be made in this connection. They will be developed as we proceed.

1. First, our understanding of God's judgment must cohere with our view of God himself. If we believe God to be a loving Father, who sent his Son to be the Saviour of the world, we cannot think of God's justice in human terms as tyrannical, impersonal punishment.

2. Secondly, it is untheological to separate (in a Marcionite manner) the God of the Old Testament from the God of the New, and presuppose that the character of the former is wrathful, while the nature of the latter is loving. An obvious difference to our knowledge of God is made by the advent of Christ, but there can be no dichotomy in the being and nature of God. He is one, and his judgment must also be one.

---

[31] A similar example, but with more limited benefits, is the blinding of Elymas (Acts 13:8–12).

That judgment, I would argue, is consistently salvific in its character and intention.

3. Thirdly, nothing that has been said so far should be taken to suggest that God's judgment is unreal. Divine justice and love belong together, but such a coherence does not imply that God's judgment is a fiction. The holiness of God cannot co-exist with human ungodliness, and this is the basic meaning of 'wrath' in the New Testament.[32] There are eternal consequences involved in trusting our own righteousness, rather than God's; for, as the writer of Hebrews says, it can be fearful 'to fall into the hands of the living God' (Heb. 10:31). Nonetheless, we need only examine the use of the term 'wrath' in the Apocalypse, to grasp its creative and positive implications. For example, the announcement that God's wrath will be poured out on those who are allied with idolatrous resistance to the church, is followed by a call for endurance and a benediction on those who die in the Lord (Rev. 14:9–13). Similarly, the winepress of wrathful anger trodden out by the Word of God, after the destruction of Babylon (Rev. 19:15), anticipates the vision of a new creation, marked by peaceful reconciliation between God and his people, and healing among the nations (Rev. 21:1 – 22:5).[33] Biblically, it may be concluded, divine justice is always real and persistently constructive.

The present section of our study also raises the issue of divine *standards*. We saw earlier that the judgment of God is defined in relation to the unrighteous being and behaviour of the human race. His perfect holiness and love and

---

[32] Rom. 1:18, et al.

[33] See further Smalley, *Thunder and Love*, 149, and the literature there cited.

justice have been finally disclosed in Jesus; and in that
light, when humanity fails to meet the divine standards, it
can only be condemned for its sinfulness.[34] God's love is
such that he wants us to be like his Son; but when we
choose to go our own way, we bring his judgment on ourselves. Divine discrimination speaks of the seriousness
with which God regards human wrongdoing; it tells us
that he is wholly opposed to selfishness, social injustice
and the ruthless exploitation of natural resources.
Although psychology and sociology may help to explain
the conditions that lead to such actions, they do not exon-
erate them. Human rebellion against God is a reality
which, by itself, precludes enjoyment of the vision of his
perfect goodness.[35]

Present Judgment

The teaching of the New Testament develops the witness
of the Old Testament writers to the nature of divine judgment by showing that it operates both in the present *and* in
the future. Christian eschatology, as we know, includes
three tenses: past, present and future.[36]

God's judgment, on earth and in the present, must be
understood as greater than the natural and impersonal
process of cause and effect; although C.H. Dodd has
argued that the category of divine 'wrath' in the Bible
should be interpreted in this way (sin is the cause, disaster

---

[34]   Cf. Rom. 3:3–7, 21–23.

[35]   Doctrine Commission, *Mystery of Salvation*, 126. Cf. Rev. 21:7–8.

[36]   See further R.E. Brown, *The Gospel According to John* (2 vols.; AB 29
and 29a; London: Geoffrey Chapman, 1971), 1, CXVI- CXXI; C.G. Kruse,
The Gospel According to John (TNTC; Leicester: Inter-Varsity Press,
2003), 153–55, commenting on John 5:24–30.

the effect).[37] There *is* a sense in which natural, and even divine, justice may be so construed. For example, if someone chooses to give higher priority to drug taking, than to working and care of the family, that individual will suffer, and so will the family. But the New Testament writers appear to understand God's judgment in personal, rather than mechanical, terms (consider, for example, such a passage as John 5:19–29). They also perceive that the phenomenon of divine discrimination operates now, as well as at the end. In this case, we may well ask how its effects may be discerned. Should individuals, or communities, fall short of God's standards, what do we expect to happen?

Such questions presuppose that divine judgment, on earth at least, will be experienced physically. It may be true that human wrongdoing leads to material suffering, and that, as we have seen, it is possible to see God's hand in such situations. Consider, for example, the symbolic paradigm of the four horsemen of the Apocalypse (Rev. 6:1–8). These four cavaliers represent *causes*: the manifestation of truths connected with Christ's kingdom, insofar as his standards judge the world. Those causes (military power, war, famine and death) are expressions of God's eschatological judgment, active in the present but anticipating the close of the age. The four riders may then be interpreted as satanic agents in this process, used by God to portray his discrimination against human arrogance, and rebellion of any kind. When power is wrongly used, that is to say, negative consequences inevitably follow. These can be experienced in a physical form. But the torment involved is fundamentally spiritual, and consists of the

---

[37] C.H. Dodd, *The Epistle of Paul to the Romans* (MNTC; London: Hodder & Stoughton, 1932), 20–24, commenting on Rom. 1:18.

agony that is brought about by conscious exclusion from a
needed personal relationship with God, through the
Lamb.[38]

Divine judgment in the present is ongoing, even if it is
not always obvious. Since the Word became flesh, and
light finally shone in the darkness, there is an inevitable
separation between those who believe and are not condemned, and those who prefer to remain in the darkness
and are 'condemned already'.[39] Such divine justice is universal, and affects not only unrighteous individuals, but
also unjust societies, and churches infected by idolatry of
any kind. However, through the grace of God there exists
the hopeful possibility of escaping that judgment. This is
not achieved by passing beyond sin into sainthood, which
seldom occurs in this life, but by making our own the truth
that inseparable from divine judgment are the Father who
runs to embrace the prodigal son (Luke 15:20), and the out-
stretched arms on the cross which are there to welcome the
penitent criminal (Luke 23:43).[40]

Future Judgment

According to the New Testament, then, God's judgment
may be experienced in the present, and on earth. In that
case, we may now consider the relation between divine
justice before death, and *after* this life. What is the nature of
'the judgment to come', as reportedly discussed, for example, by Paul in the presence of Felix?[41]

---

[38]   See Rev. 20:15; 21:8; 22:15. See also Smalley, *Thunder and Love*, 75–76;
G.K. Beale, *The Book of Revelation: A Commentary on the Greek Text*
(NIGTC; Grand Rapids & Cambridge/Carlisle: Eerdmans/Paternos-
ter Press, 1999), 370–89, esp. 388–89.

[39]   John 3:18; cf. John 1:5, 14; 3:18–21; 1 John 1:5–7.

[40]   Doctrine Commission, *Mystery of Salvation*, 126–27.

[41]   Acts 24:25; cf. Heb. 9:27 ('it is appointed for mortals to die once, and
after that the judgment'). Two main terms are used for 'judgment' in

Four points may be made about the theology of future judgment:

1. First, the New Testament view of divine judgment in the future is dynamic, and not static. So far as I can detect, the precise phrase 'The Last Judgment' is not biblical at all. Instead, the writers of the New Testament documents, like the prophets before them, speak much more readily of 'the last day (or days)'.[42] But even the term 'last', in this context, needs to be understood eschatologically, and not temporally. For 'final' judgment, or discrimination 'at the end', may mean justice encountered at the end of a person's life, or at the end of the world, or at any point in between. Final judgment has to do with consummation, and not termination.

2. Secondly, future judgment, like divine justice in the present, affects everyone. At the 'end' there will be a double resurrection: the raising to condemnation of those who have done evil, as well as a resurrection to life of those whose works have been good.[43] We must *all* appear before the judgment seat of the Father and the Son.[44]

3. Thirdly, the human perception of the nature of divine justice in the present must be applied to any understanding of God's judgment in the future. If God is known through Christ, on earth and in the church, as

---

[41] (*Continued*) the Greek New Testament: κρίσις (*krisis*) and κρίμα (*krima*). Both words are forensic in character, and their meaning is similar; although the former denotes primarily a 'judicial decision' (cf. John 5:29), while the latter may include the sense of human or divine condemnation (John 9:39; Jas. 3:1). See further F. Büchsel, 'The Concept of Judgment in the NT', *BTDNT*, 471–75.

[42] See Isa. 2:2; Mic. 4:1; John 12:48; 2 Pet. 3:3, et al.

[43] John 5:28–29.

[44] Rom. 2:6; 2 Cor. 5:10; Rev. 20:12.

loving and just and holy, the same character must be posited of his being and activity in the heavenly realm. Since God and Jesus are essentially and eternally unchanging,[45] divine judgment cannot be executed in one way during time, and in a different manner in eternity.

4. Finally, we have noticed that the writers of the Old Testament discerned a positive purpose in God's judgmental work. The same is true of the teaching about this subject in the New Testament. God's judgment is still seen to be corrective and restorative, and a positive part of the divine discipline.[46] Divine judgment, like divine love, is refining in its character and purpose. Indeed, in the phrase of Jacques Ellul, the judgment of God is the 'justice of Love itself'.[47]

The Process of judgment

Before drawing together the threads of this discussion, it will be useful to consider one further aspect of future judgment. The process of justice in human terms normally involves a distinction between passing judgment and carrying out the sentence. When a criminal is brought to court, the sentence is rarely put into immediate effect at the end of the trial, particularly if an appeal is to be made. It is possible that such a procedure may influence our conception of divine judgment, causing us to imagine that there is always an interval between God's judgment now and the execution of his sentence in the future ('at the end').[48] This

---

[45] Cf. Heb. 1:12; 13:8.

[46] Heb. 12:7–13.

[47] J. Ellul, *Apocalypse: The Book of Revelation* (New York: Seabury Press, 1977), 213. On the nature of judgment in Revelation see further ibid., 171–213.

[48] It could also be argued that the judgment, which in general forms part of God's kingdom, is fully realised after the suffering and

is undoubtedly too mechanical and impersonal a way of interpreting divine justice, and in any case it runs counter to the theology of judgment present in a Pauline passage that is of great significance for this present study.

In 1 Corinthians 4:1–5, Paul speaks about various forms of judgment. He begins by mentioning human criticism among individuals.[49] Evidently the Corinthian Christians had been making unfavourable comments about the apostle; but he regards such 'judgment', even by himself, as unimportant. This is so, Paul argues, because justice of any kind must eventually submit to the judgment of God: 'it is the Lord who judges me' (v. 4). He goes on to say that passing judgment on the human level is in any case to be avoided, since ultimately all judgment properly belongs to God, that it will take place when the Lord comes, and that everyone will be involved in it. Then Christ will 'bring to light that which is now hidden in darkness, and will disclose the purposes of the heart' (v. 5). That is to say, judgment at the end will clarify *what has been in process all the time.*

Judgment now and the final judgment are not different realities, but parts of the *same* process. Like the prophet-seer of the Apocalypse, Paul writes in the conviction that the sovereignty and judgment of God have already broken into world history, so that the present is to be interpreted in the light of its end.[50] Paul's language at this point in 1 Corinthians 4 is fascinating. The outcome of the ongoing process of divine judgment, he says, is not 'condemnation' (ἀπόκριμα, *apokrima*), as in 2 Corinthians 1:9, but rather *'commendation'* (ἔπαινος, *epainos*): 'then each one will

---

[48] (*Continued*) exaltation of Jesus. See H. Ridderbos, *The Coming of the Kingdom* (St Catharines: Paideia Press, 1978), 170–74.
[49] See also Rom. 2:1–3.
[50] Schnelle, *History and Theology*, 534.

receive commendation from God'. Final judgment means the ultimate disclosure of an ongoing allegiance (or otherwise) to Christ, and the degree of social and individual faithfulness to that allegiance.[51] The situation is one of judgment not in terms of balancing the books, but as a way of measuring human possibilities. Paul seems to be claiming that God's assessment of human endeavour, like that of any good examiner, will involve praising the best, rather than damning the worst.

The New Testament as a whole supports such a positive and salvific interpretation of God's judgment. It might be argued that the symbolism of John's Revelation seems not to do so, and that it evokes more naturally the scenes of 'last judgment' depicted by Dante and Michelangelo. Yet the theological pattern of salvation through judgment is consistent throughout the Apocalypse. War breaks out in heaven, before the Devil is toppled from power and God's sovereignty is established (Rev. 12:7–10). The saints are victorious in the end, but only because of the blood of the Lamb (Rev. 12:11). The thrones of judgment are set, before the faithful are brought to life, and Satan, Death and Hades are thrown into the lake of fire (Rev. 20:4–15). In John's vision, the white throne of divine judgment is ultimately replaced by the life-giving seat of authority occupied jointly by the Father and the Son (Rev. 20:11–15; 22:1).

The road to the coming new world is certainly through judgment, and the consummation implies the coming of the crucified and exalted Christ, and the universal acknowledgement of God as King.[52] But for members of the church who are aligned with Jesus as Lord, death will result in resurrection not only to justice, but also to eternal

---

[51] Schwarz, *Eschatology*, 393; see further ibid., 390–94.

[52] Cf. P. Prigent, *Commentary on the Apocalypse of St John* (revd edn.; Tübingen: Mohr Siebeck, 2001), 624–53.

life.[53] The day of wrath becomes a day of glory. With that hope for ever before them, the saints may boldly pray, *marana tha*, 'Come, Lord Jesus!'

---

[53] Schwarz, *Eschatology*, 394.

3

Life Beyond Death

God's Absence

In this study so far, we have been considering the nature of Christian hope, together with the ongoing reality of God's judgment. We come now to pursue further the relationship between God and his creatures, on earth and beyond death, by investigating the topic of what is traditionally referred to as 'hell'. It is possible to describe this concept as 'the absence of God', an absence that may be said to exist whenever human beings choose to remain separate from their Creator. Inevitably, some of the material in this section will overlap with what has already been discussed, and with the topic of the final chapter.

The search for truth in this area has pastoral implications. Such a sensitive issue needs to be approached with care and balance, and accompanied by love and humility. Let us first be clear what the Bible has to say on the subject of absence from God before or after we die.

In the Old Testament

At the close of the Old Testament era, it seems that four major categories of hope existed in Judaism: national deliverance, individual reward in this life, personal reward after death (although, as we have seen, this category is by no means prominent), and corporate deliverance at the end time.[1] In the later Old Testament traditions, there was a movement towards stressing the punitive judgment of God; and it was by appealing to this notion that the experience of the Exile 'could be integrated within Israel's theological understanding'.[2] The notion of divine justice now arose sharply in relation to *covenant* blessings and curses, so that either 'life' or 'death' became the consequences of Israel's faithfulness and sinfulness.[3]

One focus of God's judgmental and salvific activity *after* death, in relation to his people, may be said to lie in the Old Testament symbol of 'Sheol' (שאל, *šeʾôl*). This is an abstract concept, occurring more frequently in the later traditions of Judaism than in the earlier ones.[4] The Old Testament writers, who typically use categories of time and space to express eternal truths that are otherwise difficult to describe, understand Sheol as a 'place'. Usually, Sheol (or 'the Pit') is the neutral location of *all* the dead, a place of shadows and silence where God is not to be found;[5] although the descent of the King of Babylon into Sheol, depicted at Isaiah 14:4–17, where the shades are 'roused' to greet him (v. 9), departs from the usual stillness surrounding the image. The term Sheol is also used poetically, and without reference to death, as an epitome of remoteness,[6] insatiability,[7] the powers of evil[8] or the experience of condemnation.[9]

---

[1] Cf. D.J. Powys, *'Hell': A Hard Look at a Hard Question. The Fate of the Unrighteous in New Testament Thought* (PBTM. Carlisle: Paternoster Press, 1998), 65–106, esp. 88–89.

[2] Powys, *'Hell'*, 88.

[3] Powys, *'Hell'*, 88.

[4] Of the sixty-five Old Testament instances, fifty-five appear after 1 Kings.

[5] Cf. Job 7:9–10; Ps. 6:5; 88:4–5; Isa. 38:18, et al.

[6] Deut. 32:22; Prov. 15:11, et al.

[7] E.g. Prov. 1:12; Hab. 2:5.

[8] So Isa. 28:15; 57:9, et al.

[9] Ps. 18:5; 116:3.

In Old Testament thought, God is occasionally present with the faithful in Sheol, as at Psalm 30:3 ('O Lord, you brought up my soul from Sheol, restored me to life from among those gone down to the Pit') and Psalm 139:8 ('If I make my bed in Sheol, you are there').[10] There are also eight instances where Sheol is construed as a place of negative judgment.[11] However, the Pit is never understood directly as a place of reward, even if this may be the implication of the 'distinctions' within Sheol that are suggested in Ezekiel 31 – 32.[12] The closest approach to the idea of post-mortem bliss is to be found in the difficult passages, Psalm 16:10–11 and Psalm 49:14–15.[13]

In broad terms, nevertheless, the teaching of the Old Testament writers about life after death may be said to present Sheol as a place *apart from God*, marked by God's absence. Its real horror seems to be that all contact with him comes to an end, once existence on earth is finished. But that situation is usually prompted by human 'wickedness' in general (as at Ps. 9:17), and seems rarely to be the outcome of deliberate and idolatrous rebellion against God. Such a view of the consequences brought about by conscious sinful behaviour is more clearly seen at the close of Isaiah's prophecy; although Isaiah 66 is probably idealist and eschatological in its reference, rather than being a description of life after death.[14] This passage declares that God's judgment will come on 'all flesh' (Ps. 66:16). The rebellious, says the prophet, using a characteristic image of judgment, will suffer in unquenchable fire (v. 24), while

---

[10] See also Amos 9:2.
[11] Ps. 9:17; 16:10; 49:14–15; Prov. 5:5; 7:27; 9:18; 15:24; 23:14.
[12] Note esp. Ezek. 32:17–32.
[13] For this section see further Powys, 'Hell', 83.
[14] See further J. Muilenburg, 'Isaiah 40–66: Introduction and Exegesis' in G.A. Buttrick et al. (eds.), *The Interpreter's Bible* vol. 5 (12 vols.; New York/Nashville: Abingdon Press, 1951–57; vol. 5, 1956), 757–73.

those faithful to God's covenant will share in the hope of a new Jerusalem (vv. 2, 12–14, 22–23). The spiritual truth of this passage is clear, and parallel to the general presentation of Sheol in the Old Testament: rebellion against the sovereign Lord, in any form, leads to separation from God, while faith results in life with him.

In the New Testament

We are now in a position to turn our attention to the teaching about hell that is to be found in the New Testament. Jesus himself took over from rabbinic teaching, reflected in the intertestamental literature of Judaism, the idea of judgment by fire.[15] According to the synoptic evangelists, he warned the Scribes and Pharisees that if they were hypocritical in their religious beliefs, any proselytes they made would become 'twice as much a child of *Gehenna* (γέεννα, *gehenna*)' as themselves (Matt. 23:15). He told his disciples that nothing must be allowed to stand in the way of their entry into the kingdom of God. Better one hand in the kingdom than two in Gehenna (Mark 9:43). Jesus also clarified the importance of spiritual values. Spiritual death in Gehenna, he taught, is to be feared more than its physical counterpart (Luke 12:5).

It is necessary to understand the context of such dominical statements. 'Gehenna' was originally the valley of Hinnom, near Jerusalem, which had seen child-sacrifice[16] and later became a place where the rubbish of the city was burned. It therefore became a convenient way of referring to judgment on sin, and one that every hearer of Jesus would quickly appreciate. However, the language of Jesus about the dire consequences of rejecting his message

[15] Cf. *1 Enoch* 10:11–16; *4 Ezra* 7:35–39; *Jos. Asen.* 12:10–11, et al.
[16] 2 Chron. 28:3; 33:6.

should not be read in terms of 'hell' in the accepted sense, but rather as predictions about the awful future that awaited the nation of Israel if she rejected the way of life and peace that he was proposing. Those who persisted in the way of nationalist rebellion, rather than the radically new form of Judaism outlined in his message, would turn Jerusalem into a desolate form of its own rubbish heap. The warning came true.[17]

So far we have noticed that the teaching of Jesus in the Gospels,[18] about life apart from God, is related to the belief and behaviour of his people in the present, rather than to their status after death. God's absence, in this case, is the direct result of individual or corporate rejection of his way, as shown in Christ. When it comes to the fate of individuals beyond their death, Jesus has remarkably little to say, and he includes virtually no details about the situation of the departed. In the passages concerned, the word 'Hades' (ᾅδης, *hadēs*) is used; and this is a general term for the domain of the dead, corresponding to 'Sheol'. Thus, Capernaum will not be exalted to heaven but brought down to Hades;[19] the gates of Hades will not prevail against the church of Christ;[20] and, in the parable of Dives and Lazarus, the rich man who goes to Hades after his death is portrayed as crying out for mercy in the flames of

---

[17] So N.T. Wright, *Following Jesus: Biblical Reflections on Discipleship* (London: SPCK, 1994), 78–79. Cf. also the re-use of language and ideas from Isa. 13, referring to the fall of Babylon, in Mark 13. In his eschatological discourse, Jesus is speaking not of the collapse of the universe but of the fall of Jerusalem. See Wright, *Following Jesus*, 78. Apart from the teaching attributed to Jesus, the only other occurrence of the term 'Gehenna' in the New Testament is at Jas. 3:6.

[18] The fourth evangelist does not use the language of 'hell' to denote God's absence, but rather that of judgment and condemnation (John 3:17–20, et al.).

[19] Matt. 11:23 par.

[20] Matt. 16:18.

torment.[21] In each of these instances, the implication of the imagery is that 'hell' is a place of opposition to God and his goodness, and an abode apart from him.

Elsewhere in the New Testament, references to 'Hades' are equally restrained. In his speech on the Day of Pentecost, according to Acts 2, Peter quotes twice from Psalm 16 the Davidic hope that the Messiah would not be abandoned to Hades.[22] Otherwise, the term 'Hades' appears only in the Apocalypse of John.[23] The exalted Christ is said to possess the 'keys of Death and Hades' (Rev. 1:18); these were evidently the names of the rider of the fourth apocalyptic horseman (Rev. 6:8); and Death and Hades are finally thrown into the 'lake of fire' (Rev. 20:13–14). This symbol in Revelation, like that of the 'Abyss',[24] becomes a further, dramatic way of presenting the concept of hell. Once more, the allusion is to a realm apart from God. This is a domain associated with the fires of judgment, and with the evil and idolatrous opposition to God personified in the figures of the Devil and the satanic Beast. But it is important to bear in mind at this stage that, in John's Revelation, divine judgment on human errors of faith and conduct can never be separated from God's ultimate and salvific purposes of love.[25]

Sheep and Goats

Before leaving this section, it will be relevant as well as instructive to consider a passage in the teaching of Jesus

---

[21]   Luke 16:23; see the whole passage, Luke 16:19–31.

[22]   Acts 2:27, 31.

[23]   2 Pet. 2:4 has the equivalent word 'Tartarus' (τάρταρος, *tartaros*), which is a *hapax legomenon* in the Greek New Testament.

[24]   See Rev. 9:1–2, 11; 11:7; 17:8; 20:1, 3. Cf. also Luke 8:31; Rom. 10:7.

[25]   See Rev. 21:1–7, et al.; also Smalley, *Thunder and Love* 147–49. On the biblical subject of 'hell' generally see further H. Bietenhard, 'Hell, et al.', *NIDNTT* 2 (1976), 205–210, esp. 206–208.

that includes a rare glimpse of his description of life after death. This is the vision of final judgment in the so-called parable of the 'sheep and goats' (Matt. 25:31–46), with which the first evangelist concludes his account of the ministry of Jesus. As John Robinson says, this section 'stands out from the Gospel pages with a unique and snow-capped majesty. It is a literary *tour de force* never quite approached elsewhere' in Matthew's Gospel.[26] On the surface, its message seems straightforward. Whatever we do in this life counts in the next, so that we may be separated for judgment as easily as white or brown sheep and black goats in Palestine, then or now, may be distinguished from one another. It *is* important to feed the hungry, welcome the stranger, clothe the needy, visit the sick and care for the prisoner (vv. 35–36); but *not* to perform these acts of mercy is also crucial (vv. 42–43).

However, the very individuality of this pericope brings with it questions about its form and deeper meaning. Matthew 25:31–46 is usually known as a 'parable', although the parabolic element is confined to just two verses (32 and 33). Furthermore, this passage is not marked by the structure of a parable followed by allegorical interpretation, such as may be found in the two other Matthaean 'parables of separation', the Tares and the Drag-net.[27] Bishop Robinson has investigated the construction of this section, and concluded that its original core was an authentic, dominical parable about a shepherd separating his flock, and a set of antithetical sayings about the eschatological consequences of accepting or rejecting Jesus in the person of the outcast and helpless. Matthew's artistry then

---

[26] J.A.T. Robinson, 'The "Parable" of the Sheep and the Goats' in *Twelve New Testament Studies* (SBT 34. London: SCM Press, 1962), 76.
[27] Matt. 13:24–30, 36–43; 13:47–50. See also Mark 4:1–9, 13–20; John 10:1–18.

consisted in fusing the parable with an allegory of final
judgment, using the sayings of Jesus as the ground upon
which such judgment is given, and linking the result with
an introductory statement about the parousia of the Son of
man.[28]

The minutiae of Robinson's position need not detain us.
The point of drawing attention to it is to provide a more
critically enlightened basis on which to probe the finer
meaning of this passage, and relate it to the present topic of
life beyond death. In that case, three points may be made:

1. This pericope is unique in the synoptic Gospels
   because of its inclusion of the term 'punishment'
   (κόλασις, *kolasis*). Jesus says to those who have turned
   away from him that they will 'go away into eternal
   punishment' (v. 46). The only other use of this term in
   the New Testament is to be found at 1 John 4:18, where
   the writer claims that 'fear has to do with punishment'.[29] The Johannine quotation probably contains a
   characteristic ambivalence: John is saying that fear
   anticipates and makes real the future pain of judgment that it contemplates.[30] Interestingly, in classical
   Greek the meaning of κόλασις (*kolasis*, 'punishment',
   or 'chastisement') included the positive idea of 'discipline', rather than retribution.[31] The same notion is
   probably also present at Matthew 25:46. For the theme
   of retribution, as such, is slight in the New Testament,
   and restricted to passages that are not always clear in

[28] Robinson, 'The "Parable"', 90–91. For a similar fusion between the
parousia of the Son of man, and accountability for personal actions in
relation to him, see Mark 8:38.
[29] But see the use of the cognate verb at Acts 4:21; 2 Pet. 2:9.
[30] So S.S. Smalley, *1,2,3 John* (WBC 51; Waco: Word Books, 1984), 260–
61.
[31] For the evidence see Smalley, *1,2,3 John*, 261.

their meaning.[32] As David Powys says, 'There is no certain support within the New Testament for an expectation of ongoing conscious suffering for the unrighteous.'[33] It is perhaps significant, in this connection, that nowhere in this passage are any details offered about the nature of the 'eternal fire', or 'eternal punishment' into which the unfaithful enter (vv. 41 and 46), or indeed about the kind of bliss shared by the righteous (vv. 34 and 46).

2. The concluding, antithetical statement of the section from Matthew 25 that we are studying, in verse 46, describes an 'eternal' division. The unfaithful will be separated from the King (in 'eternal punishment'), but the righteous will go away 'into eternal life' (εἰς ζωὴν αἰώνιον, *eis zōēn aiōnion*). These categories are equal, but opposite. The unhappy lot of those who have not served Christ well on earth is contrasted sharply with the destiny of those who share the eternal quality of divine life. This is the life of the perfect and permanent kingdom of heaven, in fellowship with the Father, the Son and the saints.[34] It must therefore be regarded as the opposite of eternal death, or punishment, since this is a quality that belongs to life when it continues apart from God, or in opposition to him. In one sense, it may be suggested, 'eternal death' is the equivalent of 'hell', both before and after physical death.

3. At first glance, the 'parable' of the sheep and the goats appears to support a doctrine of salvation by works. Judgment, that is to say, seemingly proceeds on the

---

[32] Cf. possibly Rom. 2:6; otherwise, only 2 Thess. 1:5–10; Heb. 2:2; 2 Pet. 2:9; Jude 7; Rev. 6:10; 16:6; 19:2.

[33] Powys, 'Hell', 416.

[34] Cf. F.V. Filson, *The Gospel according to St Matthew* (BNTC; London: Adam & Charles Black, 1960), 268.

basis of what people have done, or failed to accomplish. The issue is then whether society or individuals have cared for the needy, or selfishly ignored them. Yet the controlling issue in this part of Matthew 25 is in fact what people have done with and for Christ. The real question concerns the depth of our relationship to him, and whether or not *for his sake* we have consciously or unconsciously put faith into action by serving, as he did, the helpless. The lesson of this pericope is then clear. To be properly 'in Christ' leads to life, whereas the faith and conduct that fail to see him in others can only result in a spiritually dead existence, and an arid life apart from God.

The Location of Hell

In the context of the present discussion, it is relevant to be reminded that life apart from God is a spiritual quality, and not a physical location. It is true that the biblical writers occasionally use a picture of the universe suggesting that it consists of three 'storeys': heaven at the top, earth in the middle and the underworld below. Thus, the Psalmist speaks of going up to heaven (Ps. 139:8), and down to Sheol (Ps. 88:4). Paul asks rhetorically who will ascend to heaven to bring Christ down, or descend into the abyss to bring him up from the dead (Rom. 10:6–7; cf. Deut. 30:11–14); and he obviously has a 'three-decker' cosmology in mind in his vision of every knee bowing to the Lord Jesus 'in heaven and on earth and under the earth' (Phil. 2:10). The writer of the Apocalypse depicts a similar cosmological arrangement from time to time.[35]

---

[35] Cf. Rev. 5:13; 10:6; 12:12; 14:7; 21:1. For 'sea', in each of these passages, as the chaotic waters under the earth, and therefore a symbol of disorder and possibly wrongdoing, see Gen. 1:2; Deut. 5:8.

Clearly, as is now well known, the universe is not organised in this way. We have also seen, from the pericope in Matthew 25, that 'eternal death', like its counterpart 'eternal life', is a quality and not a quantity. So, if hell is an eternal quality of life where God is absent, it cannot be measured, or located anywhere as a 'place'. Rather, it means being deprived at any time of divine life. Obviously, this can be the case after death; but it is also possible during life in this world. The common phrase, 'hell on earth', points to this truth. Hell is where God is *not*; and to be estranged from him in life, consciously or unconsciously, is to be already an inhabitant of the spiritual abyss.

This theological proposition may be extended to the next life. Beyond death, or at the end of the world, time and space disappear, and what remains may be the same chosen quality of spiritual apartness from God. Now, however, the 'purposes of the heart' are disclosed, and God is seen and known through his exalted Son.[36] This very situation, the vision of a Lord who is present but cannot be reached, is the real torment of eternal life without God. Despite the imagery of divine judgment as a process of 'fire',[37] there is no biblical or theological warrant for understanding eternal death as the experience of *physical* pain; indeed, in the light of our studies of hope so far, and my interpretation of hell as a *spiritual* category, this supposition presents us with a blatant contradiction in terms. The agony felt by individuals is relational: it is that of being separated from God, their Creator and Saviour. The pain affecting God, on the other hand, is that embodied in the cry of dereliction by Jesus on the cross,[38] and expressed in

[36] 1 Cor. 4:5; Phil. 2:9–11.
[37] Cf. Gen. 19:24; 2 Pet. 3:10; Rev. 20:9–10, et al.
[38] Matt. 27:46 par.

any rejection of his love. For he takes no pleasure in the death of the wicked.[39]

The Population of Hell

Given the nature of hell, a further issue at this point concerns its inhabitants. To put the question in the spatial terms that have already been deemed inadequate, 'who will go there?' It may be posited at once that the dignity and individuality of human beings is expressed in their free will; so that those who choose to live apart from God may be said to be in hell. God judges those who deliberately put themselves beyond the reach of his love. That is to say, hell is a human, and not a divine, creation.

This was true from the beginning, and applies to angelic, as well as earthly, beings. 'God did not spare the angels when they sinned', says the writer of 2 Peter, 'but cast them into hell (Tartarus), and committed them to chains (or pits) of deepest darkness to be kept until the judgment' (2 Pet. 2:4). Such a text is in line with the biblical teaching that life apart from God is the direct result of rebellion against him; although 2 Peter 2:4 seems to suggest that *God* is from the outset responsible for the imprisonment of the angels in an underworld. But this is a further example of the Judaic literary practice of regarding everything as under the sovereign control of God, so that result is treated as cause. 'The angels rebelled, therefore they chose hell', becomes 'God cast the sinful angels into Tartarus'. Life apart from God, whose nature is love,[40] is the condition of those who choose to rebel against him.

How much further may we go? Is hell *only* for those who rebel? What about the general run of non-Christians,

---

[39]   Ezek. 18:23; 33:11. Cf. further Doctrine Commission, *Mystery of Salvation*, 192–93.
[40]   1 John 4:8, 16.

the pious Muslim or Hindu or Buddhist, the devoted African traditional worshipper, or the agnostics and atheists who are sincere and good people? What about the members of our own family who are not Christian believers now, or were not before their death? And what about those who have never even heard of Christ?

Here we are on very delicate ground. But the evidence of the Bible in general, and the New Testament in particular, leads to a theological conclusion that is relevant to the total subject of life and hope beyond death. It is that God, who dispenses eternal life, is fully known through his Son, Jesus Christ, alone.[41] This is the doctrine of what Professor Charlie Moule calls the 'ultimacy' of Christ.[42] God has revealed himself in Jesus Christ in such a way that he is the unique event of that revelation, and the decisive criterion of what is meant by 'God', and his inclusiveness.[43] Christian hope rests on the faith that God has acted in love, on behalf of his creation, in Christ, and that through him alone believers may enter into true life. As a result, the abiding claim of the Christian scheme, which needs to be maintained humbly but boldly, is that, although there may be many ways to Christ, he is the way to God (John 14:6). It is because of *his* life and death and exaltation that he can be known as the Saviour of the world, and may command the allegiance of everyone.[44]

On this showing, the conclusion is plain. To know God through Jesus Christ means receiving his gift of everlasting life. Without such knowledge, however, the opposite must obtain; and this is the equivalent of eternal death.[45] In the

---

[41] Cf. John 17:3, et al.
[42] C.F.D. Moule, *The Origin of Christology* (Cambridge/New York: Cambridge University Press, 1977), 142–74; see esp. 142.
[43] Moule, *Origin of Christology*, 174.
[44] John 4:42; 2 Cor. 5:15, et al.
[45] Cf. 1 John 5:11–13.

remaining part of this discussion we need to face the obvious and implicit question. Is such a situation without qualification? If we can choose to be on one side of the line or the other in life, does the same possibility exist beyond death?

Changing Sides

The first point to be made, in answer to the last question, is that human freedom implies human responsibility. To remain absent from God is to remain apart from the life that he gives. But the *responsibility* for living apart from him depends on how much we have seen or heard. So there is a difference, I submit, between the person who chooses to live apart from God, and one who is journeying towards him, but has never discovered Christ as the way. An illustration may help to clarify that variation.

After the six-day war in June 1967, between Arabs and Israelis, many people fled from West Jordan because it was occupied by Israel. Later, some of the Jordanians who wished to return were allowed to do so, by making an application and crossing the River Jordan itself. Imagine some Arabs in that position, who were allowed to return home. Almost certainly they would have taken the appropriate steps to do so. But if, for some reason, they chose *not* to return, they would take such a decision knowing what they would be missing: family, home town, business and the rest. If, thirdly, they were among those who were not permitted to return, or had never been informed of the possibility, they could neither return, nor be held responsible for their actions.

The difference is evident. The person who knows the way, and refuses to cross the spiritual River Jordan, so to say, is more responsible than the individual who has never heard that there is a river to cross. In Pauline language, when there is no law, it cannot be violated.[46] The opportunity to know God through Christ is not always present on earth. In that case, might the opportunity be available beyond death? There is, admittedly, very little biblical evidence to suggest that it is possible for individuals to 'change sides' in the next life. But there is little warrant either for the opposite view; unless, for example, we press the unique image of the 'fixed chasm' in Hades, between the rich man and Lazarus, described by 'Father Abraham' in the parable of Luke 16.[47]

We can only ask which is more consistent with the nature of God as Jesus has revealed him: a Creator whose purposes for his creation are destructive or redemptive? The intention of God's judgment and love on earth is salvation, since he 'desires everyone to be saved and to come to the knowledge of the truth' (1 Tim. 2:4). In the life beyond this earth, anything less can scarcely be contemplated; although such a proposition is intended neither to cheapen the justice and grace of God, nor to diminish the content of Christ's gospel. Support for the inclusive nature of God's will for his creatures may be derived from the statement in Ephesians 1:10 that the divine plan for the fulness of time is to 'gather up all things' (ἀνακεφαλαιώσασθαι τὰ πάντα, *anakephalaiōsasthai ta panta*) in Christ. This is seen as the end of the entire eschatological movement: the attainment of the divine ideal by the 'heading up' of everything in Jesus Christ, when imperfection will become the final stage of perfection, and when the issue of the present spiritual conflict, already determined, will be resolved in a new creation.[48] It seems

[46] Rom. 2:12–29; 4:15; 7:7–8, et al.
[47] Cf. Luke 16:23–26.
[48] Eph. 1:11–14. See S.S. Smalley, 'The Eschatology of Ephesians', *EvQ* 28 (1956), 152–57, esp.155–57 and the literature there cited. Cf. also the vision of the new heaven and earth in Rev. 21:1–5.

that nothing is to be excluded from this gracious activity, and that no individuals will be able to escape God's salvific intentions;[49] although the universalist implications of such a claim have yet to be addressed.

Purgatory

Meanwhile, the notion of purgatory, which is relevant to the present discussion, warrants some consideration.[50] The doctrine of purgatory is a traditional feature of Roman Catholic theology. St Augustine of Hippo, at the turn of the fifth Christian century (AD 354–430), spoke in his *City of God* about the value of the church's prayers for those who die in its communion, and of a fire that purifies after death.[51] Pope Gregory the Great, in his sixth century *Dialogues*, expounded a form of this concept in order to justify liturgical prayers for the dead. A classic formulation emerged much later when, in the thirteenth century, the scholastic theologian Thomas Aquinas, known as the 'angelic doctor', taught that in purgatory unforgiven guilt is expiated, and any punishment for remaining sin is borne. The doctrine of purgatory was defined as an official part of the teaching of the Western church at the Council of Lyons in 1274, and later, at the Council of Florence, in 1439.

It was through Dante, the great Italian poet of the early fourteenth century, that belief in purgatory seems to have become 'an important part of the mental and spiritual landscape of late medieval Europe'.[52] Dante's vision of purgatory, in the second book of his *Divine Comedy*, is a

---

[49] Cf. Eph. 1:22; also Rom. 11:36; 1 Cor. 15:28.
[50] For this section see further N.T. Wright, *For All The Saints? Remembering the Christian Departed* (London: SPCK, 2003), 4–13, 20–36.
[51] *City of God* 21.24; 21.26.
[52] Wright, *For All The Saints?*, 6.

powerful symbol of the holiness that God requires from his creatures, but also of his love for them, as they are made 'pure and apt for mounting to the stars'.[53] Such sentiments also find warm expression in the *Treatise on Purgatory* by Catherine of Genoa (1494). Just before the Reformation, at the start of the sixteenth century, the idea of purgatory was central to the piety and belief of much of the Catholic Church. Masses and prayers for those in this state were common, and such a practice obviously, and sadly, became open to abuse.

The medieval doctrine of purgatory, involving punishment and purification, is one way of bridging the gap between the death of the individual and the general resurrection of the dead. It allows for what the Council of Lyons called 'full satisfaction' for human sin. The wicked will immediately pass to hell; but the saints, who are by nature unfitted for heaven, must (it is suggested) undergo a period of punitive pain before they are able to enjoy the beatific vision. If the late medieval period saw the full flowering of this belief, the late nineteenth century experienced one of its most influential literary expressions in the poem by John Henry Newman, written in 1865, which was later immortalised in the music of Edward Elgar's *The Dream of Gerontius*. The extent to which the traditional versions of the doctrine of purgatory have become modified in contemporary theology is evident from the work of such Catholic scholars as Karl Rahner and Joseph Ratzinger.[54] It is also interesting that Pannenberg himself has recently spoken of God's final judgment in terms of a process of transforming purification, *rather than* as relentless punishment.[55]

---

[53]   *Divina Commedia, Purgatorio* 33.145.
[54]   See further Wright, *For All The Saints?*, 10–11.
[55]   W. Pannenberg, 'The Task of Christian Eschatology' in C.E. Braaten and R.W. Jenson (eds.), The Last Things: Biblical and Theological Perspectives on Eschatology (Grand Rapids/Cambridge: Eerdmans,

It has to be said that biblical evidence for a theology of purgatory is almost impossible to find.[56] Section 22 of the Articles of Religion adopted by the Church of England makes the point in colourful language, by stating that purgatory is 'a fond thing vainly invented, and grounded upon no warranty of Scripture'. On the other hand, there is plentiful support in the New Testament for the notion that the work of Christ is sufficient, in response to faith and baptism, to free believers from sin in life and by the time of death, so that a progressive stage of judgment and cleansing after death and before the end becomes unnecessary.[57] Although in life we struggle with sin, and may make some progress towards genuine holiness, our inclination towards wrongdoing ends at death. In Johannine language, 'those who believe in (Jesus), even though they die, will live' (John 11:25); and, according to Paul, 'if we have died with Christ, we believe that we will also live with him' (Rom. 6:8).

The idea of purgatory, then, appears to belong to the realm of sentiment, rather than good theology. In this respect, I warm to Tom Wright's suggestion that purgatory has more to do with life here on earth, than with life after death;[58] and I also applaud his conviction that, in the intermediate state between physical death and final resurrection, there are no category distinctions between Christians. 'All are in the same condition; and all are "saints".'[59]

---

[55] (*Continued*) 2002), 1–13, esp. 9–10. See also Doctrine Commission, *Mystery of Salvation*, 196–98.

[56] But see the disputed texts at Matt. 12:32; John 14:2; 1 Cor. 15:29; cf. Wis. 3:4–5. Appeal to 2 Macc. 12.39–45 is difficult, since this passage relates to atoning offerings made on behalf of the dead in order to ensure their share in the resurrection (v. 43), rather than their release from a purgatorial state.

[57] Cf. John 13:10; 15:1–3; Rom. 5:1–2; 6:6–11; 8:1–2; Col. 2:11–15; 1 John 1:7; 3:9. Note esp. Jude 24.

[58] Wright, *For All The Saints?*, 34–35. See Rom. 8:18–25, 35–37.

[59] Wright, *For All The Saints?*, 21.

This latter point is supported by Paul's imagery in 1 Corinthians 3:10–15, which is one of the most striking passages in the New Testament about judgment at or after death. The apostle is speaking about the construction of God's church (vv. 10–11), and the difference between the Christians involved in this process. However, the distinctions to be revealed eventually refer not to growth in holiness, or closeness to God, but rather to the quality of the work carried out here and now by Christian teachers and preachers. Some are building with the best materials, such as gold and precious stones; others are working with inferior elements like wood and even straw. The final Day of the Lord will make clear the quality of the craftsmanship (vv. 12–13). Yet there is no sign here that Paul is speaking about those who will go straight to heaven, and those whose pilgrimage will be delayed by purgatory. He is saying that *all* the saints will be saved: some gloriously, others with the smell of fire still on them.[60] This is a parable about service here, and not about sanctification hereafter.

Nevertheless, there is one further, and important, point to be made in this section. It appears from the teaching of the New Testament, and especially from the Pauline literature, that it is theologically possible to speak of an intermediate state occurring between the physical death of Christian believers and their final (bodily) resurrection. So Paul, in his letter to the Philippians, says that he wishes 'to depart and be with Christ', since that is 'far better' than remaining in the flesh (Phil. 1:21–24). But he also differentiates between being 'with Christ' in heaven (Phil. 1:23), and bodily transformation, or resurrection, at the end (Phil. 3:20–21). However, this interval is not said to be occupied by a stage of purgatory; it is rather described by Paul as

---

[60] Wright, *For All The Saints?*, 25–26. Cf., similarly, the sayings of Jesus about the 'first being last' (Matt. 19:30 par., et al.).

'being asleep' in Christ.[61] This frequent imagery cannot imply that the saints are in a state of unconsciousness (living in another 'Sheol', as it were), since spiritual sleep, even more than physical, must involve growth as well as life. If being asleep in the Lord after death is 'far better' than being with him on earth, then, a new quality of existence seems to be implied.

The scene in Revelation 6:9–11 may help to illuminate such a condition. There, the souls of the martyrs are depicted as awaiting, underneath the altar, the final redemption. They are told to rest (v. 11), but they are clearly conscious, and able to ask about the establishment of God's justice (v. 10). At the same time, they do not yet share fully in the close covenant relationship, with God through the Lamb, that is to be the mark of life in the new Jerusalem (Rev. 22:1–2). We are not given much information about the abode and activity of Christians who sleep in the Lord; but we may conclude that they are not *in*active, and that they possess a marked hope of 'waking up' to resurrection life in the final new age.[62]

It needs to be added, perhaps, that the language underlying the concepts both of purgatory and sleeping in Christ depends on a temporal understanding of life beyond death. In this interpretation, it is presupposed that there is an 'interval', a period of 'waiting', between physical death and final resurrection at the 'end'. However, such a linear view satisfies the need for the human mind to understand eschatological ideas in terms of time, rather than eternity; although in Johannine theology especially, and among New Testament writers generally, earth and heaven, time

---

[61] So (in texts using the verb κοιμάομαι, *koimaomai*, 'to lie down, or be laid down, in sleep') 1 Cor. 11:30; 15:6, 18, 20, 51; 1 Thess. 4:13–15; cf. also, more neutrally, Matt. 27:52; John 11:11–12; Acts 7:60; 1 Cor. 7:39; 2 Pet. 3:4.
[62] See Wright, *For All The Saints?*, 23–25.

and eternity, are consistently presented as belonging together.[63]

God's Final Absence?

All the evidence so far surveyed seems to suggest that life with God, or apart from him, involves human choice. Final judgment remains a reality, even if its earlier depiction in punitive terms has often distorted the truth about its real and restorative nature. Just as importantly, the reality of hell, as indeed of heaven, ultimately affirms the true possibilities of human freedom.[64] We may choose God's life, which leads (as we shall see later) to heaven; alternatively, we have the freedom to remain apart from God, which is the equivalent of hell. The question then remains: is it necessary or possible to be in hell for ever?

In the history of the Christian church, three responses have been made to that enquiry. First, the universalist position, associated with Origen and gaining ground in more recent, liberal theology, maintains that everyone will eventually be saved. St Augustine vehemently criticised the universalism of Origen, particularly because his doctrine of *apokatastasis* included the restitution of Satan and his angels to the grace of salvation, thus presuming to 'oppose God's words with what purports to be a higher form of compassion'.[65] The opposite view, associated with Augustine himself, argues (notably in Book 21 of his *City of God*) for the eternal punishment of unbelievers. Asserting the

---

[63] I owe this insight to a personal conversation, on 29 July 2004, with Professor C.F.D. Moule. See further Smalley, *John*, 265–70.

[64] Cf. Doctrine Commission, *Mystery of Salvation*, 198–99.

[65] Augustine, *City of God* 21.17. Cf. further Evangelical Alliance Commission on Unity and Truth Among Evangelicals Report, *The Nature of Hell* (London: Acute, 2000), 56–57.

absolute sovereignty of God over both Christians and non-Christians, Augustine drew on such texts as Mark 9:47–48 and Matthew 25:46 to maintain what would become a familiar link between the eternity of life in Christ, and an opposite eternity for those who reject the gospel.[66]

A third, median, stance is adopted by those who espouse the more recent cause of 'conditional' salvation. This phrase describes the belief that immortality is not a necessary attribute of the immaterial soul, but conditional on its behaviour during life in the body.[67] On the other side, 'conditional immortality' implies the annihilation of those who are not saved, so that they pass beyond the reach not only of hope, but also of pity.[68]

As they stand, I do not find any of these positions (salvation as universal, as denied to the wicked, or as conditional on the behaviour of the faithful) theologically apt. In particular, I cannot accommodate the notion of the permanent punishment[69] or eternal destruction[70] of individuals within my perception of the creative and salvific nature of God in Christ. While I have sympathy with the 'conditionality' stance, moreover, the language it employs seems to obfuscate the real issues. I therefore conclude with my own version of life after death without God.

I would argue that, despite the New Testament language of 'bodily' resurrection, to which we shall return in

---

[66] Augustine, *City of God* 21.23; also 21.12–13. See Evangelical Alliance, *Nature of Hell*, 55–57; also the conclusions about hell at ibid., 132 (7–8).

[67] Earlier, only the African Christian writer Arnobius, in the fourth century, maintained this opinion.

[68] For a recent study of the fate of the unrighteous in New Testament thought see Powys, *Hell*. Note, in connection with the 'conditionalist' view of salvation, the conclusion on 416. See also Wright, *Following Jesus*, 80.

[69] So Filson, *Matthew*, 268.

[70] See Evangelical Alliance, *Nature of Hell*, 132 (9).

due course, life beyond death, both individually and corporately, should be understood primarily in a way that is spiritual and relational, rather than physical.[71] In heaven, as on earth, the quality of the relationship between God and his creatures is affected by faith, or otherwise, in his purposes of love. God is the source of everlasting light and life,[72] and to cut ourselves off from that life by choice is a form of spiritual euthanasia. It must end in death, and final separation from God; and this is the equivalent of being no more. The imagery of the new Jerusalem, in Revelation 21–22, is relevant in this context. However difficult this may ultimately become, the possibility exists eternally of having the freedom to remain outside the gates of the holy city,[73] while being aware of the blessedness of those who wish to remain within.[74]

Conclusion

None of this means, of course, that Christians are relieved of the responsibility of proclaiming the gospel faithfully in the present age.[75] Nevertheless, I conclude by submitting for your consideration the thesis that, after death, we *can* decide to escape from God's absence into his presence, and that in any case there remains a universally glorious hope for ever.[76]

---

[71] Cf. Rom. 9:19–26; 2 Cor. 5:6–15, et al.
[72] 1 John 1:5; 5:11–12.
[73] Rev. 21:8, 27; 22:15.
[74] Rev. 22:14. See further Wright, *For All The Saints?*, 44–46.
[75] Cf. 1 Cor. 1:17–18; 9:16; 2 Cor. 6:2; 2 Tim. 4:1–2.
[76] For the material in this chapter see further N.T. Wright, *Jesus and the Victory of God* (Christian Origins and The Question of God, vol. 2; London: SPCK, 1996), 320–68; also Polkinghorne, *God of Hope*, 136–38.

4

A New Creation

God's Heaven

The imagery of the New Testament, and in particular the Revelation to St John the Divine, has been determinative in the formulation of the concept of God's new creation in the theology of the Christian church, and the personal faith, literature, art and architecture which it has inspired. In his *Brief History*, Alister McGrath draws a contrast between this fact, and the approach to the subject of heaven by such a writer as Augustine of Hippo. He points out that, although Augustine's theological analysis of the idea in the *City of God* has been an important influence on Christian thought down the ages, its significance has been intellectual, rather than iconic.[1] In this section, we shall conclude our study of the biblical notion of hope by concentrating on the significant and symbolic presentation of the age to come by the writers of the New Testament themselves.

The term 'heaven' is used in the Bible in a variety of senses. It can mean the sky itself, for example, which God stretches out like a curtain over the earth, or causes to vanish like a scroll rolling itself up.[2] Heaven is also the abode of

[1] A.E. McGrath, *A Brief History of Heaven* (Oxford: Blackwell Publishing, 2003), 16–17. In Augustine's *City of God*, note esp. Books 14–22.
[2] Isa. 40:22; Rev. 6:14.

angels, and above all it is the dwelling-place of God, where he sits enthroned in sovereign power.[3] Since this spiritual realm is a divine dimension, it can describe the inheritance of Christians before and after death,[4] and may become a way of referring to God himself.[5] The word 'Paradise', which finds its background in the Creation and Fall narrative of Genesis 2 – 3, occurs only three times in the New Testament, notably in the address of Jesus to the penitent criminal on the cross;[6] and, in each case, it appears to be a synonym for 'life after death', or indeed 'heaven' as such.

Of all the biblical symbols used to describe life beyond death, those in the Apocalypse have a special and timeless resonance. The imagery of the new Jerusalem (in Rev. 21:1–22:5), for example, is particularly evocative. This theme is integrated with motifs drawn from the Creation saga, including the 'tree of life',[7] suggesting that heaven may be interpreted as a restoration of the bliss of Eden. The holy city itself represents the close, covenant relationship that exists between God and his people in eternity. The members of the church in heaven are portrayed as dwelling in a walled enclosure, spiritually protected but also possessed.[8] Angels guard the twelve gates of the heavenly city; but, unlike ancient fortifications, the gateways are open to all who wish to enter them. Moreover, in a remarkable transformation of images, the city has become a temple, where all are priests, and God through the Lamb has become all in all (Rev. 21:22).

John's eschatological vision of life after death and in eternity is essentially relational, and indeed

---

[3] Matt. 18:10; Isa. 66:1; Matt. 5:34; Rev. 4:2, et al.
[4] Phil. 3:20.
[5] John 3:27.
[6] Luke 23:43; also 2 Cor. 12:4; Rev. 2:7.
[7] Gen. 2:9; Rev. 2:7; 22:2.
[8] Cf. Rev. 7:1–17; 21:10–14.

ecclesiological, in character. The city of the new heaven and earth is strikingly portrayed as a cube (Rev. 21:16), signifying that it is a perfection of the square temple that Ezekiel saw as part of the rebuilt Jerusalem after the Exile.[9] The new city includes the restoration of the twelve tribes of Israel (Rev. 21:12–14), and thus becomes the holy space occupied by the new Israel of God.[10] We may venture one step further and say, with Augustine, that heaven has to do with love, and not just with right relationships. 'The two cities (in this world and in the next)', he maintains, 'are shaped by two loves: the earthly by self-love, even to the contempt of God, and the heavenly by the love of God, even to the contempt of self.'[11] The saving life and love of God, and our response to them, are eternally inseparable.[12]

The Descent into Hades

The 'descent' of Jesus into Hades, or the so-called 'harrowing of hell', may be considered at this point, since it concerns the state of the dead in relation to Christ before his incarnation, and the possibility of their eternal release from the underworld. This doctrine, which seeks to establish the activity of Jesus between his death and resurrection,[13] is firmly embedded in the early Christian creeds, and first appears in fourth century Arian formularies. Its

---

[9] Ezek. 43:13–17; 48:20.

[10] Cf. Gal. 6:16.

[11] *City of God* 14.28. For this section see further Smalley, *Thunder and Love*, 154–57; Beale, *Revelation*, 1039–121; McGrath, *History of Heaven*, 10–13.

[12] Cf. Doctrine Commission, *Mystery of Salvation*, 44–45.

[13] As the notion of being 'asleep in Christ' fills the period between the physical death and general resurrection of Christians, so the 'descent' of Christ into hell suitably occupies the 'interval' between the crucifixion of Jesus and his resurrection from the dead.

place in the New Testament, however, is in fact circumferential.

The idea receives indirect reference in Acts 2:27 and Romans 10:7, where the writers allude to it in the reinterpretation of Old Testament passages.[14] In two other texts, the concept of the 'descent' of the exalted Christ becomes more explicit. At 1 Peter 3:19, the context is the congruent suffering of Christ, culminating in his death, and that of the Christian. After his passion, the writer says, the Lord 'went and made a proclamation to the spirits in prison', since they had previously been disobedient. This text may be taken as a symbol, meaning that Christ, as Victor and no longer Victim, announced inclusively, and to every world of existence, his triumph and the possibility of salvation through him (vv. 20–22). This thought is continued, I would say, in 1 Peter 4:6, where the notion of preaching to 'the dead' arises from a consideration of the painfulness, as well as the glory, of being dead to sin. As in the earlier reference, what is more, the thought of judgment ('having been judged in the flesh, since everyone is judged') is subordinated to that of life ('they might then live in the spirit, as God does').

Despite its credal form, the *descensus ad inferos* is clearly an image, and not an event. Even if Peter has the idea in mind on these two occasions, and in any case, theology is more important here than chronology or geography, and the place of meaning transcends that of manner. It also fits theologically, if not literally, into the 'descent-ascent' pattern of the coming of Christ to this world, as conceived by both John and Paul.[15] The 'descent into Hades' may then be understood as part of the triumphant activity of the exalted Christ. He is Lord of hell as well as heaven, and in

---

[14] Ps. 16:10 and Deut. 30:12–13 respectively.
[15] John 6:62; Eph. 4:9–10, et al.

this symbolic manner he completes his involvement in every conceivable area of experience.[16] As such, and at all times, he offers to every believer in him the possibility of resurrection, and salvation through judgment.

A New Heaven and Earth

The concept of heaven, embracing the life that God's people will share with him beyond death and in eternity, is evidently spiritual in character: it is qualitative, and not quantitative. Nevertheless, the vision that John the Divine receives, according to Revelation 21:1, is of 'a new heaven and a new *earth*', following the disappearance of 'the first heaven and the first earth'. This text is obviously relevant to our discussion, and warrants some consideration now.

Heaven and earth belong together in biblical thought, and notably in Johannine theology, so that the renewal of the cosmos not surprisingly involves both. But it is necessary to probe the exact *nature* of this transcendent order, for which creation itself and human history have been prepared. Given that the 'first heaven and the first earth' have disappeared, this seems to involve not simply a universe freed from sin and renewed for rejoicing, as in the background of Isaiah 65 and 66,[17] but rather a completely spiritual and newly formed dimension. At one level, the thought and language of the prophet-seer seem to suggest that the '*new*[18] heaven and earth' *replace* a creation that has ceased to exist.

---

[16]   Phil. 2:5–11; Rev. 1:18. On this section see further S.S. Smalley, 'Descent Into Hades', *IBD* 1, 383.

[17]   Cf. Isa. 65:17 LXX; 66:22. See further Muilenburg, 'Isaiah 40–66', 754–55, 772.

[18]   Using the Greek adjective καινός (*kainos*, 'new', in the sense of 'unused'), rather than νέος (*neos*), meaning 'fresh', or ' renewed'.

However, in John's thought earth cannot be detached so easily from his view of heaven. The vision in Revelation 21 – 22 is of a new order that is God himself, dwelling in close relationship with his people. The holy city of liberation, the new Jerusalem, replaces the 'great' city of oppression, the fallen Babylon (chs. 17 – 18). But the connection between earth and heaven remains, and God is at work in both. The new Jerusalem, like its angel, *descends* from heaven (Rev. 21:2), while the eternal temple, which is God and the Lamb, can be described and even measured (Rev. 21:10–22).

An analogy may be found in the nature of the resurrection body of Christians, since this includes (as we saw earlier) a movement from physical death to spiritual life, without the loss of individual identity.[19] Similarly, in John's theology, there is continuity between the existence of the universe in time and in eternity; so that, while heaven and earth disappear in spatial terms, they are transfigured and differently expressed in an entirely new dimension. Yet the divinely given moral, and even material, values of God's creation, together with such abiding qualities as order, beauty, goodness and harmony, are preserved and developed. In such a setting the church awaits the final consummation, and the 'new heaven *and new earth*' continues to resonate with the uninterrupted spiritual worship of the saints, and with the joy of God's salvific light (Rev. 22:3–5).[20]

Judgment and Rewards

We have already discussed the nature of divine judgment, in relation to human existence on earth and beyond death

---

[19] See also below.

[20] Cf. Rev. 7:15–17; 21:3–7. Similarly, in the new age, the chaos induced by sin (the 'sea' of Rev. 21:1) is no more. See further Smalley, *Revelation*, 523–25 (on Rev. 21:1).

(see chapter 2). A related issue is that of 'rewards'. Does the way people live in time and space make any difference to their 'place' in heaven? The Bible gives little guidance on the subject of rewards for the righteous; although, if believers are judged after death as well as beforehand, the possibility of some kind of recognition for good works seems logical.

According to Luke 14:14, on one occasion Jesus spoke of repayment for unselfish actions 'at the resurrection of the righteous'; although this could simply be construed as meaning that every act has its consequence, and should elicit the most worthwhile response.[21] Similarly, the 'parable' of the sheep and the goats in Matthew 25 stresses the importance for the future of selfless behaviour in the present.[22] However, in general the teaching of the New Testament seems to concentrate on 'rewards' as having meaning in *this* life, rather than the next, and to understand them as the spiritual blessings that accrue from being part of the new creation 'in Christ'.[23] In any case, Christians are taught to think of themselves as 'worthless slaves';[24] they are also reminded that they live under grace, not law,[25] and that good works are important but not by themselves a means of salvation.[26] In the light of any traditional understanding of the merciful nature of God, moreover, the idea of first-class honours in heaven for the specially good seems out of place as the thought of particular punishments in hell for the extra bad. As the Saints know well, the knowledge of God is its own reward.

---

[21] So E.E. Ellis, *The Gospel of Luke* (NCB. London: Nelson, 1966), 193–94.

[22] See also 2 Macc. 7:9; Luke 20:35; John 5:29.

[23] 2 Cor. 5:17–18; Eph. 1:3–14; Heb. 12:18–24; 1 Pet. 1:3–5; 1 John 1:1–7, et al.

[24] Luke 17:10.

[25] Rom. 6:14.

[26] Rom. 3:28; Eph. 2:8–10; Jas. 2:14–26, et al.

Heaven on Earth

So far we have been considering the new creation as a theological phenomenon belonging to the future. But what about the possibility of a heavenly existence in the present? For the writers of the New Testament are well aware that the hope of eternal life is not an entirely future expectation. The church on earth is made up of those who are already 'citizens of heaven' (the Greek of Phil. 3:20 may be translated literally as 'our commonwealth[27] is in heaven'). In that case, believers who are 'in Christ' may be regarded already as part of the new creation to come.[28] Accordingly, the relationship with God that is shared by the saints in eternity becomes a projection of the same fellowship, with the Father through the Son, which has been enjoyed by them in time.[29]

Three special aspects of hope mark such a life, the existence of heaven on earth. First, there is a foundation of *resurrection hope*. We considered earlier the different senses that are included in the Christian concept of rising in Christ from death to life, which can take place at baptism, at physical death and at the end of the world.[30] Those who are baptised in true faith 'die' spiritually to sin, and 'rise again' to the new life that God gives through his Son (Rom. 6:3–11).

The baptismal liturgy in the primitive church, attested by the *Didache*, Tertullian and the *Apostolic Tradition* of

---

[27] The term πολίτευμα (*politeuma*) can denote 'a colony of foreigners'. See BDAG, 845*b*.

[28] Cf. Doctrine Commission, *Mystery of Salvation*, 195.

[29] Cf. 2 Cor. 4:16–18; 5:17; Phil. 1:6; Heb. 10:34, et al.

[30] The 'first' (and implied 'second') resurrection of Rev. 20:5 probably refers to the difference between 'sleeping' in the Lord at physical death and 'waking' in him at the consummation. For this text, and the significance of the 'millennium' (Rev. 20:2, et al.) see further Smalley, *Revelation*, 502–504, 508–510.

Hippolytus,[31] included triple immersion in the threefold divine name. This was part of a process that was striking in its symbolism. The candidates went *down* into the water to represent dying to the old life, they were immersed *in* the waters as a picture of being buried with Christ in his death, and they came *up* from the river or baptistry and put on fresh clothes as an image of their resurrection to newness of life. In this way, the church is a standing reminder of the resurrection of Christ, and of his risen life enacted in the present through the lives, the worship and the service of his followers.

A second quality of heavenly life, as it may be expressed here and now, is that of *confident hope*. The hope of the first Christian believers was confident, in that it was based on the redeeming work of God in his Messiah. The martyrs of the church, past and present, have known this confidence, because they have tasted heaven already, and anticipated eternal life beyond physical death.[32] So also Paul could speak clearly of the inheritance that would one day belong fully to the Christian church, but is shared already by its members;[33] and the writer of the Pastorals could declare, 'I *know* the one in whom I have put my trust, and I am *sure* that he is able to guard until that day what has been entrusted to him.'[34]

Thirdly, precisely because Christians are able to live out *on earth* an existence that keeps in touch with heaven, theirs is a *responsible hope*. As Paul says in Colossians 3, demands are made upon those who are 'raised with Christ' (v. 1), and therefore live in two worlds: the divine and the human. Life changes, and its values become

---

[31] The attribution is probably, but not certainly, correct.

[32] Cf. 1 John 3:16; Rev. 2:13; 6:9–11; 12:11.

[33] Rom. 8:15–25.

[34] 2 Tim. 1:12.

renewed. Renunciation is involved (vv. 5–11), but so also is acceptance (vv. 12–17). Elsewhere in the New Testament it is plain that Christians are still called to worship together and preach the gospel, as well as to resist sin and fight the good fight of faith. Social and family relationships will change for the better, honest work must continue, taxes should be paid and the authority of rulers respected. Those whose hope is 'laid up' for them in heaven[35] have an ongoing responsibility to act rightly, pursue justice and peace, and above all to obey the love-command.[36] Although the saints ultimately do not belong to this world, they are nevertheless required to behave within it as responsible citizens of their present society, as well as of the world to come (John 17:14–19).

The Inhabitants of Heaven

John depicts the character of the heavenly Jerusalem, in Revelation 21, by using the imagery of a cubic city, built of walls and foundations encrusted with precious stones; and this suggests at once the difficulty of trying to express spiritual realities by using material categories. Given that problem when describing the character of heaven, as a realm of the spirit and not a place, the task of portraying the appearance of its inhabitants becomes, perhaps, even more complex. What will God's people be *like* in the new creation? We have touched already (in chapter 1) on the nature of the resurrection body, when we noticed that there is a parallel to be drawn in part between the

---

[35] Col. 1:5.

[36] Cf. Heb. 10:25; 1 Cor. 9:16; Rom. 7:4–25; Eph. 6:10–17; 2 Tim. 2:3; Eph. 5:21 – 6:9; Col. 3:18 – 4:1; 1 Pet. 3:1–9; 2 Thess. 3:6–13; Rom. 13:1–7; 1 Pet. 2:13–17; 1 Pet. 2:11–12; Phil. 4:8; Jas. 2:1–9; Matt. 5:9; 1 Thess. 5:13; John 15:12; Rom. 13:8; 1 John 4:11, et al.

resurrection body of Christ and that of the Christian, just as there is between his resurrection and ours. We need to develop that theology at this point.

First, the resurrection body of the believer, like that of Jesus, will not be physical but *spiritual*. As Paul says, in 1 Corinthians 15:44, what is sown a physical body 'is raised a spiritual body'. The word translated here as 'body' (σῶμα, sōma) does not, of course, mean the human framework of flesh and bones, otherwise it could not be described as 'physical' in one context and 'spiritual' in another. The 'body' is a somatic totality, the core of personal being. The ambiguous phrase in the Apostles' Creed, 'I believe in the resurrection of the body', cannot be understood in purely physical terms, any more than the resurrection itself. To think of the new heaven and earth in this way is to make nonsense of the whole concept.

But, secondly, there *is* a connection. The spiritual resurrection body of believers, like that of Christ, will be *recognisable*. It will be a 'body', not in the sense of flesh and blood, but in terms of an identifiable *persona*. Instead of a personality known in time and space through physical characteristics, the body of the resurrection will become apparent in ways that are unpredictable, but no less real and recognisable. When Paul speaks of the 'kind of body' in which raised believers will come,[37] he describes the passage from the physical body to the spiritual as a metamorphosis: 'We will not all die, but we will all be *changed*' (1 Cor. 15:51). He uses an agricultural metaphor to underscore the point.[38] When a seed is sown in the ground and germinates, it becomes a plant. It does not vanish completely, but is transposed into something else. At death, that is to say, or at the end of the world, the faithful move

---

[37] 1 Cor. 15:35; see also vv. 35–50.
[38] Cf. John 12:24–25.

from the dimension of time and space to that of eternity, where essential personalities are not cut off, but differently expressed. We shall recognise each other then not by our hairstyles, but by our inner personalities.

At 2 Corinthians 5:1–5 Paul uses a further image, that of dress, to describe the resurrection body. Christians on earth, he says, are 'longing to be clothed' with their heavenly dwelling (v. 2), that is, to live with Christ in eternity. After death, therefore, they do not become 'unclothed', vanishing into nothingness, but 'further clothed', exchanging the physical for the related spiritual (v. 4). They do not take off the shirt, so to say, but put on the coat. There is a basic connection, in other words, between a personality living on earth and the same personality existing in heaven, just as there is continuity between earth and heaven themselves. But there is also a difference: that between mortality and eternal life (2 Cor. 5:4), between flesh and spirit, between time and eternity.

It is not easy, at least from the biblical evidence, to say more about the nature of the resurrection body. Christians can only declare the certain hope that, in Christ and after death, they will continue to live, and be beyond death, existing in resurrection bodies that will be not only spiritual but also identifiable. Meanwhile then, as now, what we *are* is more important than what we look like. Character is more significant than appearance. Members of the Christian church have the promise and possibility not only of imitating Christ's character closely, and becoming more like him in this life,[39] but also of being like him when they finally see him face to face.[40]

---

[39] Eph. 5:1–2.
[40] 1 Cor. 13:12; 1 John 3:2–3.

The Life of Heaven

The best way to understand and describe the spiritual realities of heaven and its membership is, like the New Testament writers themselves, to use theological tropes. Indeed, there is no other way. The same is true when it comes to making intelligible the activity of the new creation. What will the saints be *doing* in eternity? Even to pose the question in that form is to create a potential paradox, since the Pauline imagery of being 'asleep' in Christ[41] suggests *in*activity. Such a state is also echoed in Bishop Walsham How's hymn, 'For all the saints', which speaks of the 'rest' which comes soon to faithful warriors, and the 'calm' of Paradise the blest. Are we to suppose, then, that (however it be imagined) eternity is simply a quiescent dimension of repose? Let me try to address that issue by mentioning three characteristics of heaven, according to the New Testament, that suggest otherwise.

Unity

First, Christians will be together. Those who are in Christ already belong to one another, as well as to him. The same must be true after death. The biblical story is an account of God's *people*, created and redeemed and restored by him through his Son. In the Apocalypse we have an intense vision of God dwelling with his own, in the close and covenant relationship of the new Jerusalem; of the victorious company of those who have become members of a royal priesthood through the conquest of Christ; and of a vast multitude from every nation, sometimes numbered and on other occasions impossible to count, gathered around the Lord of heaven and earth, and around the Lamb.[42]

---

[41] 1 Cor. 15:51, et al.
[42] Rev. 21:2–3; 1:5–6; 7:4–9.

Here is the church triumphant, the church of God that owes its existence and character to its Lord and Saviour. The corporate character of life in heaven is marked in the theology of Revelation,[43] but not confined to it. Paul declares that *we* will meet the Lord in the air and be with him for ever; while the writer of the Letter to the Hebrews maintains that Christian believers will eventually gather in the heavenly Jerusalem, and rejoice in the presence of God as an assembly of his firstborn, enrolled eternally in heaven.[44]

The members of this assembly are all saints, in an intermediate state between physical death and bodily resurrection at the end. On earth, the term 'saint' can be used for any Christian, as in Philippians 1:1. Tom Wright believes that in 'heaven', between the resurrection at death and final consummation, there are similarly no category distinctions between Christians: all are in the same condition, and all are saints.[45] I would argue, however, that the saints in heaven are of different kinds and derivations. They have shared in varied spiritual experiences, and yet they enjoy a common faith. Some are angelic beings, some are martyrs, and most are simply 'saints', who have been sealed by God and belong to the Lamb.[46] Believers on earth are part of this same church, and belong already to a redeemed community that may be described as the body and bride of Christ, and as the family of God.[47] Christian unity here is, tragically, more often theoretical than real. But whether or not we are outwardly one, the members of Christ's church belong actively together in spirit, as they wait for the day

---

[43] Cf. Smalley, 'Johannine Community', 95–104, esp. 98–99.

[44] 1 Thess. 4:17; Heb. 12:23.

[45] Wright, *For All The Saints?*, 21.

[46] Cf. Rev. 4:6–11; 5:8–14; 7:14; 14:1, et al.

[47] Eph. 1:22–23; 5:25–27; Rom. 8:29; Gal. 4:4–7, et al.

when nothing interrupts their fellowship with each other, and with the Lord. The church on earth and in heaven is one, and also one in its potential unity.

Worship

Secondly, the church in the new creation will be engaged in constant worship. Because its members will see God as he really is in Christ, they will want to express their adoration, and say that he is worthy of all they have to offer. According to the Apocalypse, and notably in the intervals of that drama, heaven resounds endlessly with the 'new songs' of the faithful, who never tire of giving worship and praise and thanksgiving to God and to the Lamb.[48]

The liturgy offered by the saints in eternity is an extension of the worship shared in the fellowship of the church in time. God is the God of hope because he is the God of past, present and future; and it is in the sacramental, and especially eucharistic, worship of the earthly Christian community that such an eschatological hope receives a particular focus.[49] For the bread and wine of this liturgical act point to the redemptive work of God in Christ throughout history, and also foreshadow the heavenly banquet that will be enjoyed by the church when it has been gathered into God's eternal kingdom.[50]

As John Robinson points out,[51] it is in the breaking of bread above all that the church of Christ knows the presence of its risen Lord here and now. Through an open door, he comes to his own and eats with them.[52] But such an

---

[48] Cf. Rev. 5:9–10; also Rev. 5:13; 7:12; 11:17–18; 15:3–4; 19:6–8.
[49] See Polkinghorne, *God of Hope*, 100–102, esp. 101.
[50] Cf. *Didache* 9.4.
[51] J.A.T. Robinson, *Christ Comes In: Four Advent Addresses* (London: Mowbray, 1960), 28–29.
[52] Rev. 3:20.

assembly is also proleptic. Of the only two occurrences of the word ἐπισυναγωγή (*episynagōgē*, 'assembly') in the New Testament, one refers to Christians 'meeting' for worship (Heb. 10:25), and the other to the final coming of Christ himself (2 Thess. 2:1). The *parousia* of the exalted Jesus is anticipated in the first, and made real in the second.

Meanwhile, the Eucharist remains a moment of expectation. In the Lord's Supper, according to Paul, we proclaim the Lord's death 'until he comes'.[53] Nevertheless, this is not simply an act of waiting, or an empty memorial. It includes the love of God, and the active service of others; it also looks forward to the day when all sacraments will cease, and the whole of creation will be included in God's new creation.[54] In its regular acts of worship, the members of the church militant who meet together in the light of the approaching Day of the Lord[55] taste the powers of the age to come. The saints who belong to the church victorious know those sovereign powers for themselves, and rejoice to kneel before them in humble worship.[56]

Growth

The third characteristic of life in heaven to be proposed is that it is a sphere of growth. Augustine understands the eternal city of God as a realm of rest, the blessedness of which (in his view) derives from its character as a 'perpetual Sabbath'. We ourselves are the seventh day.[57] I confess that I find such an attribution difficult. If the church of the new Jerusalem, as we have noticed, lives in unity and

---

[53] 1 Cor. 11:26.
[54] Robinson, *Christ Comes In*, 29.
[55] Heb. 10:25.
[56] Cf. Rev. 5:8–14; 19:1–8.
[57] *City of God* 22.30.

engages in worship, this suggests spiritual progression: even if that idea is fashioned by temporal, rather than eternal, categories. Life in the new creation of God can only be dynamic, and not static; for where there is life there must be creativity and growth.[58]

Spiritual development is a feature of the Christian community on earth, and encouraged as part of its ongoing life. Believers are exhorted to 'grow up in every way into Christ', and to become 'a holy temple in the Lord'; and they are assured that this is possible through the Spirit.[59] As spiritual growth in Christ is an expectation increasingly realised in the church on earth, such a progression must presumably feature, in an even fuller way, as part of the vision of God. In the words of John Donne, 'I shall not live until I see God, and when I have seen him I shall never die'. In the words of John the Divine, the nations will walk by the light of God's eternal city, and 'the glory and honour of the people will be brought into it' (Rev. 21:24, 26). Although the exegesis of that passage is not easy, the sense seems to be that people will carry into the holy city *themselves*, as those who offer to God at the end-time the worship of their perpetually renewed lives.[60] Unity, worship and growth belong together in the life of the new heaven and earth.

* * * * *

The End

We need to gather up our reflections on the Christian doctrine of hope by giving some consideration to its

---

[58] Note, Rev. 21:6; 22:2, et al.
[59] Eph. 4:15–16; 2:21–22; see also 2 Thess. 1:3; 1 Pet. 2:2; 2 Pet. 3:18.
[60] Cf. Beale, *Revelation*, 1094–101; Smalley, *Revelation*, 558–60.

fulfilment. What exactly do we expect to happen at the 'end' of the ages, at the consummation?

It might be thought that, in the light of the theological ideas we have been surveying, little room is left for a future, final stage of God's judgmental and salvific purposes for his creation. Spiritual death and resurrection from death, divine judgment in the light of Jesus the Messiah, and entry into the absence or presence of God, occur on earth and in eternity all the time. Why is it necessary to go further, and speak of finality beyond this, particularly when for over two millennia such an end to the world has been expected but not realised? Why not ask with the scoffers, 'Where is the promise of his coming? For ever since our ancestors fell asleep, all things continue as they were from the beginning of creation!'[61] Furthermore, an eschatology that contains a present existence with a future climax oddly appears to be chronological and linear, rather than spiritual and eternal, in its essential character.

Nevertheless, biblical theology in general seems to include the belief that the cosmos, and history as we know it, will reach a definite point of termination. In Judaism, for example, an 'end' of some kind, involving the triumph of righteousness, was anticipated.[62] The New Testament is more precise, even if the first Christians construed the idea of an expected 'Day of the Lord' in a variety of ways. That expectation of the early church appears to have included three convictions, each of which in fact contains a different aspect of the same truth about eternal hope. These beliefs may be presented in the form of three statements.

First, *the world will come to an end.* The New Testament writers seem firmly to have anticipated a final conclusion to the universe, as we know it, including the course of

---

[61] 2 Pet. 3:4.
[62] Zech. 14:1–9, et al.

human history within it. They frequently expressed this faith by using the imagery of a coming 'Day of the Lord', which was a figure taken over from Judaism, but now associated with the advent of Jesus the Messiah. Such a future climax, according to the synoptic tradition, featured in the teaching of Jesus himself, who told his disciples to expect not only the destruction of Jerusalem in the near future, but also in due course a cosmic catastrophe, and the 'passing away' of heaven and earth.[63]

The 'Day' itself was interpreted elsewhere in the New Testament as a moment of final judgment, for individuals and for society. When it occurs, the heavens will suddenly disappear with a loud noise, the elements will be dissolved, and the earth and all its activity will be burned up.[64] Further, the 'Day' of the Lord was understood as a time of renewal, since the saints could also look forward to 'new heavens and a new earth, where righteousness is at home' and, as we have seen, to new life within the new creation.[65]

However, the theological concept of the 'end' of the world, and of its history, should not be taken to signify the end of everything contained in them. As in John's Apocalypse, the end in one sense remains perpetually elusive. Ultimately, history does not come to a conclusion but reaches its goal, when its character and purpose may be perceived from an eternal perspective. It is like reaching the end of a book, and looking back over it to appreciate its plan and contents, before taking up the sequel and continuing to read. Creation, and all that takes place within it, is at that stage released from its 'bondage to decay'; and, with

---

[63] Mark 13:31 par.

[64] 2 Pet. 3:10; some MSS read 'disclosed' for 'burned up'. For the 'Day of the Lord', as essentially a time of judgment, see also John 5:28–29; Acts 17:30–31; Rom. 2:5, 16; 1 Cor. 1:8; Phil. 1:6, 10; 2 Thess. 1:10; 2 Pet. 2:9; 1 John 4:17; Jude 6; Rev. 6:17; 16:14.

[65] Cf. John 6:39–40; 2 Pet. 3:13; Rev. 21:1, 6, et al.

the children of God, it then enters the 'glorious freedom' which God has intended for both (Rom. 8:18–25).[66]

A second promise belonging to Christian hope at the end is that *Christ will appear*. This expectation also featured in the life of primitive Christianity, and apparently stemmed from the teaching of Jesus himself. He promised, for example, that the Son of man would come 'in clouds, with great power and glory', and take his own from the four winds to be with him.[67] There was uncertainty about the time, place and manner of the final coming of Jesus. Like the kingdom of God and the 'Day of the Lord', indeed, his advent always seemed to be 'at hand'.[68] But that it would eventually occur, and coincide with the end of the world and the triumph of righteousness over sin and death, seems to have been undoubted.

This point may be clarified by taking account of the thesis about the *parousia* of Christ put forward by John Robinson. In his book, *Jesus and His Coming*,[69] Bishop Robinson challenges the doctrine, built into the New Testament and the Creeds of the church, that there is to be a '*second* coming' of Jesus at the end of the world. He believes that Jesus himself looked forward to the final consummation of the messianic age in a crowning judgment of God, in which he would share, without expecting a second act in history, after an interval, incorporating elements of visitation and vindication not introduced by the first.[70] It was members of the early church, Robinson maintains, who split the unity

---

[66] See further Schwarz, *Eschatology*, 387–90, esp. 390. He notes that the disclosure of this new world began in the resurrection of Jesus Christ, whom Paul understands as the goal of creation (Col. 1:16).

[67] Mark 13:26; Matt. 24:30–31; Luke 21:27.

[68] Mark 1:15; Jas. 5:8.

[69] J.A.T. Robinson, *Jesus and His Coming: The Emergence of a Doctrine* (London: SCM Press, 1957).

[70] Robinson, *Jesus and His Coming*, 150–51.

of Christ's climactic *parousia* in two, redacting accordingly the record of his teaching in the New Testament.[71]

That synopsis is greatly over-simplified, and does scant justice to a monograph that is based on sound scholarship, and supported by brilliant argumentation. My purpose in mentioning it is to draw attention to the conclusion, since it is relevant to our present study. A future and final 'coming' (παρουσία, *parousia*) of Christ to the world in victory is unquestionably a part of New Testament faith.[72] But those who recorded it never used the phrase, '*second* parousia'. As John Robinson says, the wholeness of the Christian hope is to be found in the unity of Christ's coming in the past and future, but also in the present.[73] He came at Bethlehem, and he will come again in glory;[74] but, through the Spirit, he also comes to his church today, even as its members wait for him. These manifestations are part of the same advent of God in Christ, although there is an important difference between them. Jesus came in the past, and comes in the present, to this world of time and space; but his 'final' appearance in majesty will be experienced in the realm of eternity.

The third element belonging to the church's hope, at the end of the ages, is an assurance that *the kingdom of God will be established*. The kingship of God is eternal, and his people have always worshipped him as Lord. The affirmation of the Psalmist, for example, 'The Lord is king for ever and ever',[75] is echoed by major and minor Old Testament prophets alike.[76] The hope of Israel for the

---

[71] Robinson, *Jesus and His Coming*, 151–59. See also Gloege, *Day of His Coming*, 277–78.

[72] See 1 Thess. 4:13 – 5:11; 5:23; 2 Thess. 2:1–12; 2 Pet. 3:3–12; Jas. 5:7–8; 1 John 2:28.

[73] Robinson, *Jesus and His Coming*, 158–85.

[74] Cf. Phil. 2:4–11; Rev. 1:5–7, et al.

[75] Ps. 10:16.

[76] See Isa. 33:22; Jer. 48:15; Mic. 2:13; Zech. 14:9; Mal. 1:14, et al.

arrival of a messianic rule, marked by deliverance and peace,[77] was fulfilled in the advent of Jesus the Christ, who inaugurated on earth the eternal kingdom of heaven.[78] As a result, Paul could speak of God's victory, already won through the cross of Christ, over the powers of evil in the world.[79]

Nevertheless, the sovereignty of God has not always been acknowledged, and the powers of evil continue to exercise their influence on individuals and society. John's vision in Revelation, therefore, is of a time when the kingdom and righteousness of God will be fully established, and when the saints who have followed him through Christ will be finally vindicated.[80] The worship of heaven is accordingly offered to God not only as Creator and Saviour, but also as King.[81] In my view, the 'thousand years' of Revelation 20 is a precise symbol of that kingship, exercised by God over his creation and its inhabitants, both in time and in eternity.[82]

---

[77] As at Dan. 2:44–45; Zech. 14:16; Tobit 13:1–17; *1 Enoch* 84:2–4; *Psalms of Solomon* 17, et al.

[78] Mark 1:15; Luke 17:21; John 18:36–37, et al. See further N.T. Wright, *The New Testament and the People of God* (Christian Origins and the Question of God, vol. 1; London: SPCK, 1992), 302–320; Wright, *Victory of God*, 198–243.

[79] Col. 2:13–15.

[80] Rev. 7:10; 11:15–17; 19:1–8. Cf. also Eph. 1:10.

[81] Rev. 4:11; 5:9–14; 15:3–4.

[82] See Smalley, *Revelation*, 502–504. Similarly, the doctrine of Christ's 'descent into hell' may be regarded as a theological trope that expresses the announcement to the universe of Christ's triumphant and salvific Lordship. See above. For a different, post-millennial, approach see W.J. Grier, *The Momentous Event: A Discussion of Scripture Teaching on the Second Advent and Questions Related Thereto* (Belfast: Evangelical Bookshop, 1945), esp. 83–90.

Postscript

We have come to the end of our thinking about Christian hope, and the character of the life to come. Often, in these explorations of life and death from a biblical point of view, it has been difficult to reach definite conclusions. Perhaps a measure of uncertainty belongs to our subject because of its very nature. As Professor John Polkinghorne says, in the book with which we began, in many cases the appropriate response must be, 'wait and see'.[83] Yet it is still possible to wait with a hope that is positive and confident, because it is grounded in the eternal faithfulness of God, who raised the Lord Jesus Christ from the dead. The gospel is incomplete without such hope for ever.[84]

---

[83] Polkinghorne, *God of Hope*, 138.
[84] Rom. 8:24–26; 1 Cor. 15:19–20. Cf. Polkinghorne, *God of Hope*, 138–39.

Bibliography

Bauckham, R. (ed.), *God Will Be All In All: The Eschatology of Jürgen Moltmann* (Edinburgh: T&T Clark, 1999)

Beale, G.K., *The Book of Revelation: A Commentary on the Greek Text* (NIGTC; Grand Rapids & Cambridge/Carlisle: Eerdmans/ Paternoster Press, 1999)

Bietenhard, H., 'Hell, et al.' in C. Brown (ed.), *The New International Dictionary of New Testament Theology* vol. 2 (3 vols. Grand Rapids/Exeter: Zondervan/Paternoster Press, 1975–78; vol. 2, 1976), 205–210

Brandon, S.G.F., *The Judgment of the Dead: The Idea of Life After Death in the Major Religions* (New York: Scribners, 1967)

Brown, R.E., *The Gospel According to John* (2 vols.; AB 29 and 29a; London: Geoffrey Chapman, 1971)

Büchsel, F., 'The Concept of Judgment in the NT' in G. Kittel and G. Friedrich (ed.), *Theological Dictionary of the New Testament* (abbr. G.W. Bromiley; Grand Rapids/Exeter: Eerdmans/ Paternoster Press, 1985), 471–75

Cullmann, O., *Christ and Time: The Primitive Christian Conception of Time and History* (London: SCM Press, 1951)

Doctrine Commission Report, *The Mystery of Salvation: The Story of God's Gift. A Report by the Doctrine Commission of the General Synod of the Church of England* (London: Church House Publishing, 1995)

Dodd, C.H., *The Epistle of Paul to the Romans* (MNTC; London: Hodder & Stoughton, 1932)

Ellis, E.E., *The Gospel of Luke* (NCB; London: Nelson, 1966)

Ellul, J., *Apocalypse: The Book of Revelation* (New York: Seabury Press, 1977)

Evangelical Alliance Commission on Unity and Truth Among Evangelicals Report, *The Nature of Hell* (London: Acute, 2000)

Filson, F.V., *The Gospel according to St Matthew* (BNTC; London: Adam & Charles Black, 1960)

Gilbertson, M., *God and History in the Book of Revelation: New Testament Studies in Dialogue with Pannenberg and Moltmann* (SNTSMS 124; Cambridge and New York: Cambridge University Press, 2003)

Gloege, G., *The Day of His Coming: The Man in the Gospels* (London: SCM Press, 1963)

Grier, W.J., *The Momentous Event: A Discussion of Scripture Teaching on the Second Advent and Questions Related Thereto* (Belfast: Evangelical Bookshop, 1945)

Hebblethwaite, B., 'The Impossibility of Multiple Incarnations', *Theology* 104 (2001), 323–34

Hoskyns, E.C. and Davey, F.N., *Crucifixion – Resurrection: The Pattern of the Theology and Ethics of the New Testament* (ed. G.S. Wakefield; London: SPCK, 1981)

Idowu, E.B., *African Traditional Religion: A Definition* (London: SCM Press, 1973)

King, N.Q., *Religions of Africa: A Pilgrimage Into Traditional Religions* (New York/London: Harper & Row, 1970)

Kruse, C.G., *The Gospel According to John* (TNTC; Leicester: Inter-Varsity Press, 2003)

McGrath, A.E., *A Brief History of Heaven* (Oxford: Blackwell Publishing, 2003)

Moltmann, J. *Theology of Hope: On the Ground and the Implications of a Christian Eschatology* (New York: Harper & Row, 1967)

Moule, C.F.D., *The Origin of Christology* (Cambridge/New York: Cambridge University Press, 1977)

Muilenburg, J., 'Isaiah 40–66: Introduction and Exegesis' in G.A. Buttrick et al. (eds.), *The Interpreter's Bible* vol. 5 (12 vols.; New York/Nashville: Abingdon Press, 1951–57; vol. 5, 1956), 149–773

Pannenberg, W., *Systematic Theology* (3 vols.; Grand Rapids: Eerdmans, 1991–98)

——, 'The Task of Christian Eschatology' in C.E. Braaten and R.W. Jenson (eds.), *The Last Things: Biblical and Theological*

Perspectives on Eschatology (Grand Rapids/Cambridge: Eerdmans, 2002), 1–13

Polkinghorne, J., *The God of Hope and the End of the World* (London: SPCK, 2002)

Powys, D.J., *'Hell': A Hard Look at a Hard Question. The Fate of the Unrighteous in New Testament Thought* (PBTM; Carlisle: Paternoster Press, 1998)

Prigent, P., *Commentary on the Apocalypse of St John* (revd edn.; Tübingen: Mohr Siebeck, 2001)

Ridderbos, H., *The Coming of the Kingdom* (St Catharines: Paideia Press, 1978)

Robinson, J.A.T., *Jesus and His Coming: The Emergence of a Doctrine* (London: SCM Press, 1957)

——, *Christ Comes In: Four Advent Addresses* (London: Mowbray, 1960)

——, 'The "Parable" of the Sheep and the Goats' in *Twelve New Testament Studies* (SBT 34; London: SCM Press, 1962), 76–93

——, 'What Future for a Unique Christ?' in *Where Three Ways Meet: Last Essays and Sermons* (London: SCM Press, 1987), 9–17

Schnelle, U., *The History and Theology of the New Testament Writings* (London: SCM Press, 1998)

Schwarz, H., *Eschatology* (Grand Rapids/Cambridge: Eerdmans, 2000)

Seebass, H., 'Holy' in C. Brown (ed.), *The New International Dictionary of New Testament Theology* vol. 2 (3 vols. Grand Rapids/Exeter: Zondervan/Paternoster Press, 1975–78; vol. 2, 1976), 223–28

Selwyn, E.G., *The First Epistle of St Peter* (London: Macmillan, 1949)

Smalley, S.S., 'The Eschatology of Ephesians', *EvQ* 28 (1956), 152–57

——, 'Descent Into Hades' in N. Hillyer (ed.), *The Illustrated Bible Dictionary* vol. 1 (3 vols.; Leicester: Inter-Varsity Press, 1980), 385

——, *1,2,3 John* (WBC 51; Waco: Word Books, 1984)

——, *Thunder and Love : John's Revelation and John's Community* (Milton Keynes: Nelson Word, 1994)

——, 'The Johannine Community and the Letters of John' in M. Bockmuehl and M.B. Thompson (eds.), *A Vision for the Church: Studies in Early Christian Ecclesiology in Honour of J.P.M. Sweet* (Edinburgh: T&T Clark, 1997), 95–104

——, *John: Evangelist and Interpreter* (2nd edn.; Carlisle: Paternoster Press, 1998)

——, *The Revelation to John: A Commentary on the Greek Text of the Apocalypse* (London: SPCK, 2005)

Whybray, R.N., 'Genesis' in J. Barton and J. Muddiman (eds.), *The Oxford Bible Commentary* (Oxford/New York: Oxford University Press, 2001), 38–66

Wright, N.T., *Following Jesus: Biblical Reflections on Discipleship* (London: SPCK, 1994)

——, *The New Testament and the People of God* (Christian Origins and the Question of God, vol. 1; London: SPCK, 1992)

——, *Jesus and the Victory of God* (Christian Origins and the Question of God, vol. 2. London: SPCK, 1996)

——, *The Resurrection of the Son of God* (Christian Origins and the Question of God, vol. 3; London: SPCK, 2003)

——, *For All The Saints? Remembering the Christian Departed* (London: SPCK, 2003)

**For a full list of the Didsbury Lectures titles
see the end of this book.**

Holy Land, Holy City
*Sacred Geography and the
Interpretation of the Bible*

Robert P. Gordon

ISBN: 1-84227-277-2

What connections exist between the physical
geography of Israel and the spirituality of biblical
faith? How was the physical space conceived as
sacred space?

In a wide-ranging study Professor Robert Gordon
leads the readers from the Garden of Eden to
Jerusalem, from Genesis through the Psalms and the
gospels to Revelation, and onwards through the
patristic period, the Middle Ages and the nineteenth
and twentieth centuries. Chapters one to four
concentrate on Old Testament texts and themes
relating to the 'holy land, holy city'. History, as well as
geography plays a part here. Gordon shows in
particular how topography of Jerusalem and its
environment have been used in diverse ways in the
spirituality of Jews and Christians over the centuries.

Chapters five through to nine begin with 'The
Geography of Golgatha' and progress into the
prophetic envisioning of the end-time pilgrimage of
the nations to Jerusalem. The vexed question of land
disputes between Israel and the Palestinians is also
considered. *Holy Land, Holy City* offers a current and
contemporary reading of sacred geography in the
Bible.

What has Infant Baptism done to Baptism?
An Enquiry at the End of Christendom

David F. Wright

ISBN: 1-84227-357-4

What has infant baptism done to baptism? What are the long-lasting effects on the understanding and significance of baptism? Beginning with New Testament teaching on the subject, David Wright presents a searching critique of the traditions of earlier centuries to the present. He shows how the contemporary shift towards infant baptism is directly connected to the emergence of Christendom, and examines the effects that this has had on the practice, theology and liturgy of baptism.

When Will These Things Happen?
A Study of Jesus as Judge in Matthew 21 – 25

Alistair Wilson

ISBN: 1-84227-146-6

This study seeks to allow Matthew's carefully constructed presentation of Jesus to be given full weight in the modern evaluation of Jesus' eschatology. Careful analysis of the text of Matthew 21 – 25 reveals Jesus to be standing firmly in the Jewish prophetic and wisdom traditions as he proclaims and enacts imminent judgement on the Jewish authorities then boldly claims the central role in the final and universal judgement.

The Didsbury Lecture Series

1979   F.F. Bruce
Men and Movements in the Primitive Church

1980   I.H. Marshall
Last Supper and Lord's Supper
ISBN: 1-84227-307-8

1981   J. Atkinson
Martin Luther: Prophet to the Church Catholic

1982   T.F. Torrance
The Meditation of Christ

1983   C.K. Barrett
Church Ministry and Sacraments

1984   A.R.G. Deasley
The Shape of Qumran Theology
ISBN: 0-85364-786-0

1985   D. Guthrie
The Relevance of John's Apocalypse

1986   A. Skevington-Wood
Revelation and Reason

1987   A.F. Walls
The Making of the Nineteenth-Century Missionary

1988   M.D. Hooker
Not Ashamed of the Gospel

1989   R.E. Clements
Wisdom in Theology

1990   C.E. Gunton
Christ and Creation
ISBN: 1-84227-305-1

1991   J.D.G. Dunn
Christian Liberty

1992   P. Bassett
A Redefinition of Heresy

1993   D.J.A Clines
The Bible Today

1994   J.B. Torrance
Worship, Community and the Triune God of Grace

1995   R.T. France
Women in the Church's Ministry

1996   R. Bauckham
God Crucified: Monotheism and Christology in the New Testament
ISBN: 0-85364-944-8

1997   H.G.M. Williamson
Variation on a Theme: King, Messiah and Servant in the book of Isaiah
ISBN: 0-85364-870-0

1998   D. Bebbington
Holiness in Nineteenth-Century England
ISBN: 0-85634-981-2

1999   L.W. Hurtado
At the Origins of Christian Worship: The Context and Character of Earliest Christian Devotion
ISBN: 0-85364-992-8

2000   C.H. Pinnock
Most Moved Mover: A Theology of God's Openness
ISBN: 1-84227-014-1

2001   R.P. Gordon
Holy Land, Holy City: Sacred Geography and the Interpretation of the Bible
ISBN: 1-84227-277-2

2002   H. McGonigle
Wesley as a Practical Theologian
(Title to be confirmed, forthcoming)

2003   D. F. Wright
What has Infant Baptism done to Baptism?: An enquiry at the end of Christendom
ISBN: 1-84227-357-4

2004   S.S. Smalley
Hope For Ever: The Christian View of Life and Death
ISBN: 1-84227-358-2

2005   N.T. Wright

2006   A. Sell
Non-Conformist Theologians
(Title to be confirmed, forthcoming)